Wild GOOSE COUNTRY

Wild GOOSE

COUNTRY

Michael Furtman

NorthWord
PRESS, INC
Box 1360, Minocqua, WI 54548

"Many people, like me, have become 'goose addicts,'
and the craving can only be satisfied
out on the wild marshes at dawn, or dusk,
or by moonlight. There is, I believe, no permanent
cure for the habit, but then I have not met anyone
who would wish to be cured."

—Sir Peter Scott, *"Wild Chorus"*

© 1992 Michael Furtman
Published by:
NorthWord Press, Inc.
P.O. Box 1360
Minocqua, WI 54548

ISBN 1-55971-177-9

Edited by Greg Linder
Designed by Russell S. Kuepper

For a free catalog describing NorthWord's line of books
and gift items, call toll free 1-800-336-5666.

Printed in Singapore.

CREDITS
Front and back cover photographs: Scott Nielsen
Front jacket flap photo: William K. Volkert
Back jacket flap photo: Jack Rendulich

Interior photographs:
Michael H. Francis, pp. 2, 72, 81
Lynn M. Stone, pp. 4-5, 16, 18-19, 22, 25, 29, 35, 41, 42, 45, 46, 53, 56, 58, 59, 79, 83, 96,
98, 99, 106-107, 110, 111, 127, 128, 130, 138, 142, 151, 152, 156-157
Scott Nielsen, pp. 7, 8, 10, 11, 13, 14, 20, 24, 26, 28, 31, 32, 34, 36, 38, 48, 49, 50, 55, 60, 61,
65, 69, 70, 71, 75, 76, 80, 84, 85, 90, 91, 92-93, 95, 100-101, 103, 109, 112, 113, 114, 116,
119, 120, 133, 134, 137, 140-141, 145, 148-149, 150, 155, 159
Jack Rendulich, p. 9
Robert W. Baldwin, pp. 62-63
Michael Furtman, pp. 66, 124-125, 135
William K. Volkert, pp. 86, 123
Wisconsin Department of Natural Resources, p. 104

Illustration
Renee Graef/Cooperative Extension Publications, University of Wisconsin-Extension, p. 64

Maps
Mary Shafer, pp. 87, 89

Library of Congress Cataloging-in-Publication Data

Furtman, Michael.
     Wild goose country / by Michael Furtman.
        p.   cm.
     ISBN 1-55971-177-9 : $39.99
       1. Geese--North America.   2. Geese--Saskatchewan.   I. Title.
QL696.A52F88   1992
598.4'1--dc20

                           92-16504
                               CIP

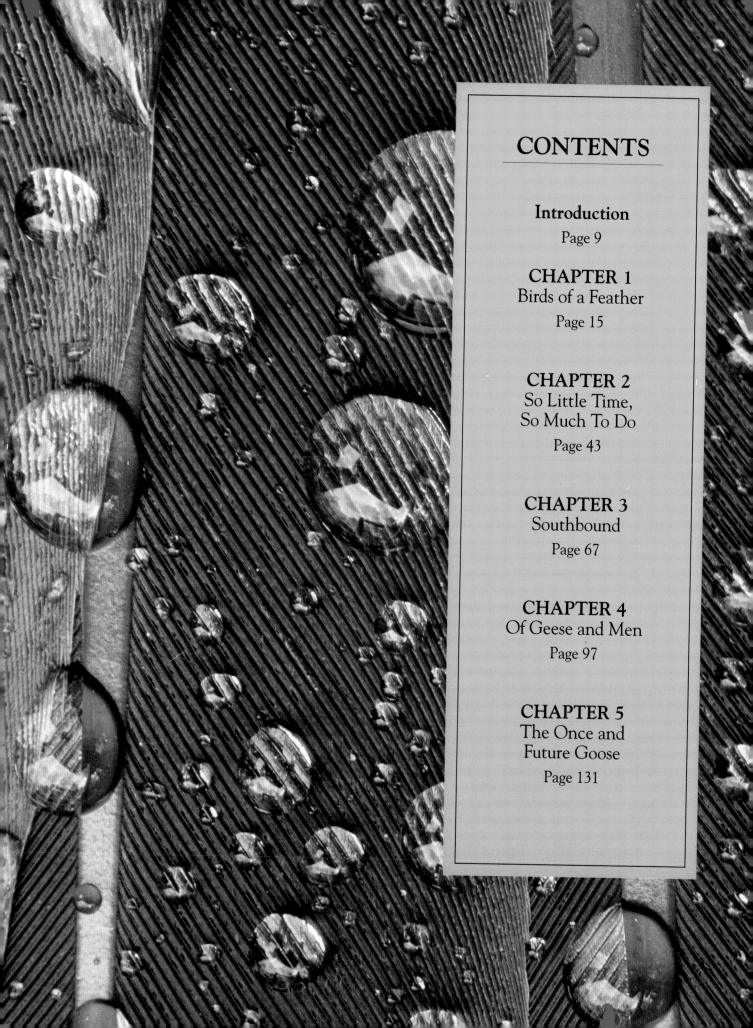

CONTENTS

THE WILD GOOSE

They came from the north in full cry. Geese. By the thousands. In the gathering darkness, against the orange glow of a Saskatchewan prairie sunset, a sinuous succession of geese flowed.

The air was full of their talk. The barking discourse of snow geese. White-fronted geese laughing. Canada geese honking in traffic. To each species' call there was a joyousness, a sense of relief, and they made the somber prairie come alive.

Rascal, my labrador retriever, sat near me. She was aquiver. I shivered, too. The air was cold; an October evening with a north wind that had come fresh from the tundra. The air was electric; filled with the sight and sound of 10,000 southbound geese. A broad, shallow prairie lake seemed to stretch from us to the sunset, and geese of all types "slipped air," spilling it from beneath their wings, dropping to the lake's surface, happy for rest and water.

We watched as night swallowed day. The lake's surface became black with the dark forms of geese. Water lapped quietly at our feet, the sound nearly drowned by the raucous procession before us. A few ducks swam near, dipping to feed, while a half-dozen sandpipers waded stiffly along the shore. Soon it

Author Michael Furtman and his labrador retriever Rascal, both fascinated by waterfowl, have traveled the length of the continent so that Furtman could watch, study, photograph, and write about geese.

was too dark to see even these, but the gathered mass of geese on the lake was evident by the music; calmer, quieter than before as they settled in for the night, but still a din.

I creaked to my feet, chilled knees protesting. Rascal and I strolled to our nearby campsite and its warmth, while coyotes yipped to the east in the aspens. Perhaps they too were thrilled to see the geese, thoughts of a goose dinner on their minds.

• • •

Geese are magic. They appear out of nowhere, coming on a schedule only their own, marking seasons, marking years, marking eons. They have done this before, made their grand migrations, flowing from the subarctic or the prairie, flying over great plains, mountain ranges, and down ocean coasts, calling, and with rowing wings eating miles, drinking vistas. They will do it again. Each spring, each fall, heralding the change in weather, brightening our human day, feeding our wanderlust and provoking our imagination, evoking our excitement and envy, twice yearly they

LEFT: Geese enrich our lives merely by engaging in their daily routine of flying and feeding, providing song and natural majesty.

In all goose species, males assist females during nesting and brooding by rigorously defending the pair's territory and offspring from interloping geese and predators.

give us pause to stop and wonder.

We humans have been wondering about geese for a very long time. Geese appear in our mythologies, our fairy tales, our languages. From a time before calendars, we knew our seasons by the geese, telling us to prepare for winter or to plant our crops for summer. They have fed us, clothed us, made us almost painfully conscious of how earthbound we are. They are one of this world's richest legacies.

It's one thing to know about the legacy as we sit at home, reading a book and marveling at photos. Yet it has almost forever struck me as mysterious that geese and I (or geese and you, for that matter) can come together at a single point on this entire globe to share the same space and time, however briefly.

I had driven two days from my Minnesota home to the wheat desert of Saskatchewan and suddenly, camped as I was beneath the twisted, stunted prairie aspens, Rascal and I were there with the geese. In my travels I had seen mostly wheat and blacktop roadways. In *their* travels the geese had seen tundra, stunted taiga, great rivers and broad lakes, hordes of caribou, native people's villages and, finally, this wide prairie lake amidst the wheat stubble, where they would rest and feed until uncontrollable urges drove them south. Theirs was, and likely forever will be, the grander journey.

So there we were, together. A little miracle of time and relativity. The geese would stay until prodded by weather, instinct, or both. We would stay a while, too; to watch and photograph the birds, to hunt them for a few meals. We would share this space and wonder, as people elsewhere had done and wondered, as people will.

Gods have appeared to us in the form of geese. They have brought gifts and messages while in this form. If geese have enriched our myths and imaginations, they have also enriched our languages. To the Ojibwa natives the goose was known as "wawa." They gave us Wawa Lake in

The glint in her eye belies the reason that humans are so fascinated with geese.

Minnesota and the burg of Wawa, Ontario. Goose Lakes abound in Minnesota, Wisconsin, and Ontario. And when our skin dimples with the rush of fright or thrill, we owe the geese for what the Cajuns call *peau d'oie*, or "goose bumps"—resembling the skin of a plucked goose that's headed for the roasting pan.

Then there's "as loose as a goose," "crazy as a goose," and "a wild goose chase." The last item, I can from experience guess, stemmed from the difficulty involved in actually killing a wary wild goose. For whomever coined the phrase, and for modern goose hunters, this surely involved a whole lot more chasing than killing.

The fact that geese can suddenly just appear in our lives has been a wonder for us from the beginning. Though we may not stop to think twice when a small warbler flits nearby, we do when hundreds or thousands of great, squawking birds appear high above us, bound for where we know not, coming from a place we've never been. To early humans,

whose scope of the world was limited to that which they had walked across in their own time, such comings, goings, and gatherings must truly have seemed miraculous. Not knowing what the broader world is like, how could they explain a marsh full of geese that, only the day before, was full of silence?

Those whose disposition leans to anthropomorphism are enamored because geese stay with one mate for most of their lives—a quality we theoretically have in common, although geese appear to be more successful at monogamy than our own race. Geese do indeed mate for life, although there are exceptions to the rule and it is strictly a myth that they pine away unto their death at the loss of a mate. They take another mate. Still, we imagine that they mimic us, rather than the other way around.

The mating distinction is one way that geese differ from ducks—but it's an important distinction that has much to do with the manner in which genetic information is spread amongst the species, as we shall see later. Ducks, geese, and swans all belong to the same family, Anatidae, and all share many common characteristics. But during the Oligocene era some thirty million years ago, geese separated from most other types of waterfowl, and they have been diversifying ever since. While their close relatives, the swans, have evolved six species worldwide, geese have divided into 15 global species—plus dozens of races and subspecies that occupy special geographic niches. Of the goose species, all but one reside in the northern hemisphere. The lone exception is Australia's Cape Barren goose.

In North America we are blessed with nine species of geese, some obscure and some well-known. We are most familiar with the Canada goose. Many know the sight and sound of snow geese—the lesser snow (and its blue phase variant) of the continent's interior, and the greater snow goose of the east coast. Fewer know the laughing white-fronted goose, or the tiny, snow-goose-like Ross' goose. Those who frequent the shores of the Atlantic Ocean have perhaps seen the swift, dark Atlantic brant; counterparts hunting or observing the

flyway of the Pacific shores have watched the similar black brant. Few of us, however, have ever seen, or perhaps even heard of, the strikingly beautiful emperor goose of Alaska, and almost no one could identify the most rare of North American geese that breeds on Cook's Inlet in Alaska, the tule goose, a larger, darker version of the white-fronted goose.

In recent decades science has begun to classify, study, and manage the geese of our continent. None of this serves to weaken our passion for geese, for with our increased understanding of these waterfowl and their needs comes an increased appreciation of their beauty, their adaptability, and their grand migrations. And the mystery is intact.

I know that. So do you. For even as I stood on the shores of that prairie lake, watching tens of thousands of geese descend for the night, and even though I knew from where they came, it was still beyond my comprehension to understand all they had seen, all they had done, all they had struggled against.

In the dark, with the sound of geese in your ears, science means little. But the magic remains.

RIGHT: All waterfowl belong to the family Anatidae. This Canada goose, as well as all other species of goose, swans, and whistling ducks, are then categorized under the subfamily Anserinae.

CHAPTER ONE

BIRDS OF A FEATHER

For many people who have little contact with nature, ducks, geese, and swans may seem to be succeedingly larger and differently colored versions of each other. That is, I suppose, where taxonomy probably began—by observing the obvious differences.

To even the casual observer, the differences between the species of waterfowl become apparent with just a slightly closer look. Size is only one distinction. Body shape, feeding methods, food preferences, mating behavior, and physiology all serve as ways to determine the species. As is the wont of science, definitive distinctions are used to classify waterfowl, and while some argument is still waged about the number of subspecies of various geese, major classification is standardized.

There was a time, eons ago, when a primordial goose may have existed—a sort of progenitor of all geese. This bird's progeny, and its progeny's progeny, would strive through the ages to adapt to new habitats as populations expanded and spread to new areas, or as changing climate forced changes in behavior or physiology. One great marvel of nature is how species evolve to fit niches, making many small adaptations over long periods of time.

Evolution has given our world richness and diversity. Diversity gives our world resilience; if all geese were alike, all could become extinct quickly due to a change in habitat or temperature or the coming of a mortal disease. But because geese, and life forms in general, have found unique niches across broad ranges, no single tragedy can cause the type of disaster just described. Diversity is strength; evolution ensures diversity.

Just as there may have been an ancestor

of all geese, an ancestor might have existed even further back in time that was the prototype of all waterfowl. At a point in time unknown—but thought to be in the early Cenozoic period some 50 million years ago—the earliest forms of waterfowl appeared, most likely having evolved to survive in semi-aquatic environments, separating through the misty ages from fowl-like birds that were land-based.

To this day, waterfowl and upland fowl retain characteristics belying their common ancestry. Both produce young that are well-developed upon hatching and able to feed themselves quickly after leaving the egg. Both generally tend to their young as a family unit, or brood, until the young are ready to fly, also known as fledging. And both use a complex vernacular of calls to alert the family to danger or to keep family members together.

Except in a few instances, though, upland fowl are not prone to migration. Perhaps the dependence of waterfowl on water, which of course can freeze, marked the beginning of migration, as these birds sought ice-free conditions during the cold months. However the split between the types may have happened, fossil records exist from the Cenozoic to prove the presence of early waterfowl. Not much else is known about them.

We do know that, as these birds evolved, the waterfowl with which we're now familiar came into existence. Some 140 species of ducks, geese, and swans populate the world today, comprising the family known as Anatidae. Five species of waterfowl belonging to this family have become extinct during historical times.

Just as ducks, geese, and swans evolved

LEFT: A telltale feather left behind by a goose that was pushed south by frost, ice, and the coming winter.

This tundra swan is a member of the genus *Cygnus*: swans are the nearest relatives of geese.

and separated over the ages, science in its evolution has separated the birds into precise classifications. Based on both common and distinct traits and behaviors, the structure of classification resembles a many-branched, upward-reaching tree. Since all waterfowl belong to the same family, Anatidae, the trunk of the tree is so labeled. But up the tree a distance (in terms of time, about 30 million years ago) the trunk forks into two distinct branches: the subfamily Anatinae, which includes virtually all ducks; and the subfamily Anserinae, which includes the whistling (or tree) ducks, swans, and all geese.

While the duck side of the family tree continues to subdivide into five tribes and numerous species, the Anserinae side splits into just two tribes, one comprised of the whistling ducks and the other, Tribe Anserini, including swans and geese.

Swans and geese, then, are each other's nearest relatives. Swans belong to the genus *Cygnus*, and geese are classified into two genera, *Anser* and *Branta*. Some features common to both geese and swans include the fact that plumage is nearly identical in both sexes. Ducks, on the other hand, display vastly different plumage in the two sexes, with the male often tending toward the gaudy.

Geese, like swans, mate for life. It's a fallacy, however, that a goose that has lost its mate will mourn unto death. Generally, the unlucky goose will choose a new mate with the coming of the next breeding season.

Perhaps because of their long-term bond, geese and swan parents share the duties of caring for young. Bonding between ducks is quite fleeting, and once the pair splits up each sex faces different risks. Since female ducks are often vastly outnumbered by males, it's probably safe to conclude that the female's nesting and rearing activities are more hazardous, leading to more frequent demises and the subsequent population imbalance.

The goose seems to fare better, since she has the assistance of her gander. If a fox attempts to raid a nest, it must face both goose and gander. If a storm whips down on the nesting grounds, both sexes are subjected to it. Thus, the geese populations are more evenly split between males and females.

Because ducks select new partners each year, they have developed elaborate nuptial rituals. One could easily speculate that drake ducks are adorned with vividly marked and colored plumage in order to enhance the nuptial display and increase the odds of attracting a mate. Conversely, the hen tends to be drab. She needs to be. Left to fend for herself and eventually her brood, the single-parent female duck must be a mistress of camouflage in order to escape hungry predators. Because geese are larger and stronger and remain in pairs, they have somewhat less need for secrecy during incubation, and are more capable of defending a nest against creatures that would consume eggs or young.

Compared to ducks, geese are relatively slow to mature sexually. While it's not uncommon for one-year-old ducks to breed, geese do not reproduce until at least their second year. The majority, in fact, wait until their third season.

Most geese are very comfortable on land, and are excellent grazers. The land-based species of geese—notably the varied subspecies of Canada goose and the lesser snow goose—are very adaptable birds, especially when it comes to wintering habitat and conversion to feeding on agricultural grains rather than native seed sources. That conversion has changed some migration behavior, and has actually accounted for the relocation of entire wintering flocks.

All waterfowl molt—that is, they replace their flight feathers each year not long before the autumn migration. However, geese and swans molt just once each year while ducks, the males adding fancy feathers for their nuptial display, molt twice per year.

Geese are different than swans in a number of ways. Though the two are cousins, the trumpeter swan could no more graze a wheat field with a Canada goose than could the Canada subsist on a strictly aquatic diet. Because they're equipped with longer legs and with bills designed to strip seeds from stems, geese in a grain field can move about easily and can quickly consume vast quantities of seed. Perhaps because geese exist on the same plane as their primary food, their necks are shorter than those of swans, which must submerge their heads on serpentine necks to gather 20 pounds daily of aquatic vegetation.

All waterfowl have gradually diverged, based largely on the survival skills needed for geographical or ecological niches. Each has become a specialist, each adept and yet bound within the range of its adaptability.

Classifying Geese

The truck came to a stop just below the crest of a wind-swept North Dakota prairie ridge. Long, grey grasses lay eastward in the cool October wind. Wind-driven dust gave the air a distinctly alkaline taste. In the low, leaden sky, geese fought the gale, their cunning wedge repeatedly ripped asunder as

OVERLEAF: Most goose species have evolved to be efficient on-land grazers. Consequently, they have readily adapted to feeding on farm crops.

individual birds were forced from the group's formation.

We watched through binoculars. The dark birds were Canada geese, and as they neared we could hear the familiar "ker-honk" of their chatter. Long necks craned this way and that, watching us, watching everything, as the big birds fought their way south. We had surprised them by parking behind the low hill; had we been hunting, the geese would have passed within shotgun range—one of the few times in all my years afield that I had seen geese make such a mistake.

But they were safe. We were just watching, touring the somber Dakota prairie, content on this day to marvel at the migration. One of my partners spoke from beneath his riveted binoculars as the geese flared at our presence. "Oh, boy. Those weren't just little grunts. Those were the big ones."

My friend was referring to the fact that these Canada geese (let's get it straight right here—they're *always* called Canada geese, never Canadian) were members of one of the large subspecies, some of which can weigh nearly 20 pounds. The "little grunts"—the small races—barely surpass large mallard ducks in size.

As it turns out, the common Canada goose is a champion of sorts, a champion of subspecies. No other goose has divided itself into so many subspecies—eleven. They're distinguished primarily by nesting location and size, for they all sport the familiar black head and white chin strap.

But before enumerating the subspecies of Canada geese, we need to address all species of geese in North America. Science has a specific manner of naming species, and while taxonomical discussions can be dry, we need to understand the language of taxonomy so we can be clear in our dialogue.

Given the difficulty of pronouncing Latin, it's no wonder that it has become a dead language. But since familiar names can change with location and are rarely specific enough to identify subspecies, science relies on Latin names to categorize all life forms, our geese included.

The method is simple. The first name, always capitalized, denotes the genus of the species. Geese are divided into two genera, *Branta* (which refers to geese with black heads and necks), and *Anser*. The uncapitalized specific (species) name follows. For instance, a Canada goose would be classified as *Branta canadensis*.

When specifying a subspecies, a third and also uncapitalized name follows. *Branta canadensis maxima* tells us we are speaking of the largest of all Canada geese, the giant Canada. And so it goes.

In North America, the genus *Branta* includes all Canada geese, as well as both species of brant—the Atlantic and black. *Anser* includes all the rest: tule, emperor, lesser snow, greater snow, Ross', and the white-fronted goose.

All of these species share many common traits, but each has evolved into a specialist of sorts. Whether by choice of food or choice of nesting habitat, North American geese have sought to fill every remotely suitable habitat on the continent.

NORTH AMERICAN GEESE

White-Fronted Goose

White-fronted geese, or "specklebellies" as they are often known to hunters, are a medium-sized (about six pounds), dark goose common to the skies of the Central and Pacific flyways. *Anser albifrons frontalis* adults have a pinkish bill; the bill of an immature is yellowish. Adults have orange legs, while immature whitefronts sport yellowish legs. When the bird is on the wing, it's very difficult to distinguish the immature white-front from an immature blue phase

LEFT: The giant Canada goose is classified as *Branta canadensis maxima*.
Branta indicates a goose with black head and neck; *canadensis* means Canada goose species; and *maxima* tells us that the goose being described is of the giant subspecies.

snow goose. But close at hand, the white-front's yellowish legs and bill differentiate it from the grey of the immature blue goose.

All white-fronted geese are grey-brown over most of their upper back, neck, and head, although mature specimens display a white face patch. The light grey chest, broken by irregular dark brown and black bars, is responsible for the "specklebelly" appellation. Their tendency to be very vocal and their riotous, high-pitched "kow-yow" has given them yet another name—the laughing goose. Those who have stood enthralled on a prairie or have hidden in a goose blind and heard the distinctive call of the specklebelly will not soon forget its chortling voice. Additionally, white-fronted geese are often ranked as the finest of table fare by those who consume goose flesh.

Various races of the white-fronted nest in subarctic regions around the world except in the Canadian northeast. North American populations nest primarily in Alaska and nearby portions of the Yukon and Northwest Territories, and in the central Canadian arctic. Of the 200,000 Pacific Flyway white-fronted geese, nearly 80,000 nest on the Yukon Delta; it's the single most important breeding ground in North America. While this population heads down the West Coast, other nearby breeding groups such as those that set up house on the Iditarod and Innoko rivers, the Arctic Slope, and the Alaskan interior populations migrate down through central Canada and the U.S., eventually wintering near the Gulf

White-fronted geese (*Anser albifrons frontalis*) are medium-sized geese common to the Central and Pacific flyways.

Coast of Texas and Louisiana. A few groups even continue on to Mexico. Those choosing the troubled, diminishing marshlands of California's Central Valley first stop in the Klamath Basin, where they gather in astonishing numbers in late October and early November before completing their journey.

Astounding as it may seem, when the rest of the Alaska geese depart for Texas, they first fly from their arctic nesting grounds to staging areas in the south of Alberta and Saskatchewan, a virtually non-stop trip of up to 2,000 miles.

The remaining population of white-fronted geese nests in the more central region of Canada's arctic—from the north-west side of Hudson Bay westward to a large colony on Queen Maud Gulf. These geese pass due south in their fall migration, flying nearly non-stop to Whitewater Lake in Manitoba and the national wildlife refuges on the Souris River in North Dakota. At this point they join forces with the western population and travel together the remainder of the distance to the wintering grounds.

Most whitefronts are early migrants, appearing in the Klamath Basin as early as the first week in September or in North Dakota by mid-month. By the last week in September, the first specklebellies are tumbling out of the sky to rest in the marshes of Texas, setting up house for the remaining whitefronts that will arrive before another four weeks have passed.

While the migration south is a grand affair of large flocks, white-fronted geese straggle north in relatively small bunches, following the receding winter. Those really anxious to get north to the breeding grounds begin to depart in February, and by the end of March the geese are well on their way to the arctic. Of course the real reason geese depart south for the winter is to avoid harsh, freezing temperatures and the invariable lack of food. While lollygagging in Texas and

California, white-fronted geese have readily adapted to consuming agricultural grain products.

Once on the wintering grounds, these geese disperse into small groups, generally comprised of a family or two. They often feed with Canada geese, but rarely do they mingle with snow geese. Their favorite food is now rice. Other grains of choice include wheat, corn, milo, and barley. Historically, whitefronts dined on panic grass, saw grass, sedges, the rootstocks of bulrushes, and wild millet. These foods still make up an important part of their diet when available. During their months in the far north, their diet remains the same as it has for centuries, probably consisting largely of sedges and horsetail.

Come late May or early June, the white-fronted geese are back to their arctic nesting grounds, searching the warming tundra for their own natal nesting area. Strong homing instincts lead them back, and they arrive in family units that include the mated pair and any surviving offspring from the previous year. This family structure persists longer in whitefronts than in other species of geese.

Whitefronts are solitary nesters. While other species gather in large nesting colonies, specklebellies prefer to spread out. Areas of highly favorable habitat may contain many of these geese, but the birds will be thoroughly dispersed. After the long flight north, the mated pair will select a nesting site in tall grass near a tidal slough, in sedge marshes, or in upland areas near interior streams and inland lakes. A nest is made of plant material, and the hen proceeds to lay her clutch of buff-colored eggs. Normally the hen will deposit four or five eggs and incubate them herself over a 23- to 25-day period.

Once hatched, the goslings are led to water within their first day of life, and the male begins to dominate the chore of caring for the brood. During this process, the non-breeding yearlings serve guard duty, flying out to waylay intruders and predators. Young whitefronts will be able to fly within about 45 days. During this same period, adult birds undergo a 35-day molt and by the end of August, all are ready to begin the flight south.

The population of whitefronts appears stable and in no immediate danger. Since accurate surveys have been in place, the white-fronted goose has generally shown population increases in the mid-continent, while slowly declining in the Pacific Flyway.

Tule Goose

Anser albifrons gambelli is a rare goose that appears to be a larger, darker version of the white-fronted goose. Statistical evaluation of many specimens reveals that the tule goose is larger in more than just weight. It's about a pound heavier than the whitefront; it also has larger feet and a longer body, bill, legs, and wings. To most of us, however, the difference between the two races might easily be lost.

The nesting grounds of the tule goose were discovered rather recently as biology goes. In July of 1978 an Alaskan biologist employed by the state, Daniel Timm, collected four specimens of the bird in Cook Inlet's Redoubt Bay, some 100 miles southwest of Anchorage. This group is the only known breeding population, and it's probably comprised of about 1,000 birds.

Tule geese migrate south in small flocks

The rare tule goose (left) is a very near relative of the common white-fronted goose (right).
The tule goose is larger, darker, and nests only in Alaska's Redoubt Bay.

and winter in California, mingling with their near relatives, the whitefronts. The total size of the wintering population is not known, but considering that their nesting success and mortality rates should be similar to those of the white-fronted, tules probably number near 2,000, and the number appears to be stable.

Lesser Snow Goose

Sometimes science screws up. For many decades, scientists thought that the lesser snow goose and the blue goose were separate species. The blue goose was accurately described by the term "dark-blue goose," or *Chen caerulescens*. The lesser snow goose, now known as *Anser caerulescens caerulescens*, was formerly classified as *Chen hyperborea*, which translates to the wonder-fully romantic "goose from beyond the north wind." It's a great name that's a shame to lose, but the name isn't accurate.

In the Northwest Territories, on the shores of Foxe Basin to the west of Baffin Island, the nesting grounds of the blue goose were discovered in 1929, after a seven-year search by Canadian ornithologist Dewey Soper. The discovery seemed to offer conclusive proof of the separate species theory. But as other colonies were discovered over the decades, researchers noted that many "snow geese" were nesting right next to "blue geese," and that mixed mated pairs occurred. For decades it was assumed that these were closely-related geese, capable of interbreeding but still distinct. However, in 1961, Dr. Graham Cooch proved that the blue goose is

The abundant lesser snow goose (*Anser caerulescens caerulescens*) nests near the arctic from the west shore of Hudson Bay across Canada to Alaska and winters in the three western flyways.

a color variant of the lesser snow, and that they are indeed the same bird. Both are now classified as *Anser c. caerulescens*—the lesser snow goose.

Both white and blue phase snow geese have pink bills and rose-red legs when mature. Both have grey legs and bills when immature. In both color phases, the sexes are nearly identical in plumage; the mature white phase is brilliant white with glossy black wing tips, while the immature white tends toward sooty gray. A mature blue phase snow goose can be strikingly beautiful, with a slate-grey body and a white head and upper neck. Such specimens are often referred to by hunters as "eagle heads"—a reference, no doubt, to the white head of the mature bald eagle. As noted earlier, the immature blue looks much like an immature white-fronted goose—almost entirely brown-grey with a lighter underside.

Snow geese are not overly large—most specimens weigh between five and six pounds. Nonetheless, they're powerful fliers; I have witnessed them plow steadily through a ferocious 40-mile-per-hour North Dakota head wind on their way to feed in the wheat stubble fields. Magnificent when traveling in huge flocks of a thousand or more, they fly in constantly changing waves—hence their common name, "wavie." On 28-inch wings they move very rapidly, more quickly than Canada geese, and their wing beat is nearly as rapid as that of some large ducks.

In flight, snow geese chatter constantly—more so than any other waterfowl. Theirs is a short, barking sound, a high-pitched yelp; they sound as if they're mimicking the war whoops heard in old western movies.

The majority of lesser snows nest in the Canadian arctic, but a few spread west into Alaska. A number nest on Wrangel Island, off the shore of Siberia, and these birds comprise a large percentage of the snows that winter in California. Unfortunately, the Wrangel population has suffered serious declines since the mid-1960s due, it seems, to poor nesting success because protracted snow cover has lasted into the summer breeding season.

On the whole, though, lesser snows are doing quite well. In recent decades the trend has been upward for the snow goose, and there may be as many as two million of them continentally during the winter (when population assessments are done), even after the hunting season. The largest colonies nest in the eastern Canadian arctic, mostly in two huge conglomerations—one on Baffin Island numbering in excess of a half-million geese, and another colony of similar size on the west coast of Hudson Bay, on and near the McConnell River delta.

Interestingly, the majority of snow geese in the Baffin Island colony are of the blue phase, as are the geese inhabiting colonies on Southhampton Island, which is midway between the Baffin and McConnell colonies. At McConnell, though, the majority are white phase, and from that point westward the blue phase is quite rare. The same holds true for the autumn migration—blue geese are rare west of the eastern Great Plains, while the two phases commonly mix east of the Great Plains.

Censuses indicate that the mid-continental population has shown an increase in the proportion of blue phase snows in recent times. Weather conditions favoring one colony over another during the breeding season may account for the proportional fluctuation.

The coastal marshes of Texas and Louisiana have historically hosted the majority of snow geese during the winter, with the white phase settling to the west and the blues to the east. Two things have changed dramatically in the last couple of decades. First, the color phases seem to mingle more freely now

LEFT: Once thought to be a separate species, the "blue goose" is now recognized as a color phase of the lesser snow goose.

The blue phase lesser snow goose (dark with white head in adults) is easy to distinguish from its white relatives.

than in the past, to the point that the distribution has become fairly uniform. Second, fewer and fewer geese are utilizing the coastal marshes, choosing instead to winter on the rice fields of Texas, Louisiana, and occasionally even Arkansas. During December, some groups can be found as far north as Missouri, Nebraska, Kansas, Iowa, and Oklahoma. The food available in the agricultural fields is certainly an attraction, and salt water intrusion into coastal marshes due to oil exploration and canals has seriously diminished the once-vital marshes. These two factors may be enough to explain the shifting trends. In any case, no one knows for sure these days where snow geese will end up in the winter.

Coastal populations of lesser snows do exist, with the Pacific Coast hosting a much greater number, comprised entirely of the white phase. Less than 2,000 lesser snows, mostly blue phase, winter on the Atlantic seaboard. Their presence appears to be a relatively recent trend, and they may drift as far south as Florida. The Pacific Flyway, however, sees many hundreds of thousands of snow geese coming from both the troubled Wrangel Island flock and the western Canadian arctic. The majority of these birds winter in California's Central Valley.

Snow geese migrating through the more easterly corridors of the Mississippi Flyway travel nearly non-stop from their staging area on James Bay to Louisiana, a distance of 1,500 miles. Perhaps because there's an abundance of open land and grain fields, snow geese flying south through the Canadian and

Though the two color phases of lesser snow geese can and do interbreed, they generally prefer to mate with birds of their own color; white geese produce white offspring, blue produce blue.

American prairies now stop at intervals to rest and feed, a recent phenomenon.

Most mass migrations take place at night. Flying at heights of 2,000 to 3,000 feet, snow geese often maintain a speed of 50 miles per hour for sustained periods. The spring flight north is an anxious affair, and the hurried snows often fly north beyond the region where snow and ice has melted, only to temporarily retreat. By mid-to-late February, the geese head for the nesting grounds, the male leading the female, halted only by inclement weather or the lack of bare earth and ice-free lakes. Their impatience seems to cost them, for they make the flight south in a shorter time. The northerly migration is a hop-scotch affair performed as winter recedes.

Depending on which arctic nesting ground they call home, the lesser snow geese arrive anywhere from mid-May to early June. Even then, they wait impatiently for the remaining snow to melt. Since the arctic summer is short, their impatience seems justified; they have only a brief time in which to raise a family and prepare for yet another journey south.

As colony nesters, lesser snows will tolerate other nesting pairs as near as 15 feet. Pairs bond at two years old, but birds three years old and older usually do the breeding. Mating takes place on the flight north. When they arrive, the mated pairs stake out their territory and vigorously defend it, while the yearlings seek water nearby to wait out the summer.

Nest sites are located near shallow lakes or rivers, on flat tundra plains usually within a few miles of the ocean. Nests are used year after year, and are made of gravel, moss, grass, willows, and down from the goose's breast. In this nest the mother generally lays an egg a day for four days, although some nests contain up to ten eggs. Most lesser snow geese populations complete egg-laying by the second week in June. Females rarely leave the nest during incubation, and they may lose a quarter of their weight. Some have been known to starve to death while performing their duties during periods of inclement weather. During this time the male stands guard against predators.

The eggs hatch in just over three weeks. While the goslings are growing, the adults molt. By the time the young are 45 days old, they attain flight; this is only a few days after the parents and the other adults have completed their molt. The geese have just barely managed to beat the clock, for migration south will begin by early September.

Despite the continued loss of wetlands in the U.S., which are important for snow geese as rest areas and wintering grounds, the snow goose population continues to grow. Man has not yet infringed upon the arctic nesting grounds, and the geese have proven adaptable enough to switch to other food sources, primarily domesticated grains, during the winter.

Greater Snow Goose

Unless you held a white lesser snow goose in one hand and a greater snow in the other, chances are you'd not be able to distinguish between them. And even then, the difference might not be apparent.

Anser caerulescens atlantica, the greater snow goose, is so like the white phase of its smaller cousin that only its slightly larger body and longer bill give it away. Both have brilliant white plumage and shiny black wing tips when adults, and the immature greater snow is as sooty as its young cousin. The greater snow weighs a pound to a pound and a half more than the lesser snow, something you're not likely to be able to measure as they fly by. There is no blue phase to the greater snow goose

You're not likely to see the two races together on the wing. The greater snow is an Atlantic Flyway goose, and only rarely do the few lesser snows that show up on the Atlantic Coast mingle with the more numerous greaters. Greater snow geese don't mingle with lessers on the breeding grounds, either. No goose—indeed, no bird—nests as far north as the greater snow, except possibly the Atlantic brant; the greater's breeding takes place largely north and east of the lesser's. In fact, one colony on Axel Heiberg Island is less than 800 miles from the North Pole!

Major breeding areas for the greater are located on northern Ellesmere Island and Bylot Island, northeast of Baffin Island. Perhaps a thousand greater snows nest on Greenland's far northwestern coast.

The majority of these big white geese winter on the Atlantic seaboard, from New Jersey to North Carolina, where they spend the winter eating the shoots and rootstocks of bulrushes. Like the lesser snow goose, the greater has in recent years taken to eating agricultural crops inland. During the autumn migration, nearly the entire population of greater snows pauses through October on the Saint Lawrence River near Cape Tourmente. Because much of their migration takes place over a sparsely inhabited region of Canada, little else is known about the particulars of their journey.

The geese pause again on the St. Lawrence River as they make their way north in late May, after leaving their wintering areas in March and April. By early June they are again in their colonies preparing to

RIGHT: The greater snow goose (*Anser caerulescens atlantica*), which nests in the eastern Canadian arctic and travels the Atlantic flyway, is less numerous and only slightly larger than the lesser snow goose.

nest and, losing no time, they deposit four or five eggs during the second and third week of that month. Much of their nesting behavior is similar to that of the lesser snow goose.

About two dozen days will pass before the eggs hatch, and shortly afterward the entire adult population begins its molt. During this period the parents move their broods inland to feed, then gradually return to the coast as the young attain size, arriving just in time for the young of the year to make their first flights. The adults have by then completed their molt. It's now the third week in August, and some of the non-breeding subadults have already departed for warmer climes. Within three weeks, the remaining greater snows will follow.

As with lesser snow geese, the popula-tion trend has been generally upward, but not without occasionally severe setbacks. Nesting so far to the north, greater snow geese are particularly subject to the vagaries of weather; in some years the nesting grounds are inundated with snow so late into the season that entire colonies simply fail to breed. In years when the lemming popula-tion is at a low, arctic foxes appear to target snow geese, which may greatly reduce their nesting success rates.

Ross' Goose

The diminutive *Anser rossii* is easily mistaken for a white snow goose because its plumage is nearly identical; however, its juvenile plumage is a considerably lighter grey than that of immature snows.

Scarcely bigger than a mallard, Ross' geese (*Anser rossii*) are nearly identical in appearance to snow geese.

Only three to four pounds in size, the Ross' goose barely outweighs a well-fed mallard. The truly observant, though, may notice that the Ross' has a more rapid wing beat and a higher-pitched call than the snow goose.

The Ross' goose has a limited breeding area. With a few exceptions, it's confined to the Queen Maud Gulf area in the central Canadian arctic. Ross' geese also use low islands on tundra lakes for nesting sites when these are available. Such locations probably afford them a measure of protection from the arctic fox.

Like white-fronted geese, Ross' geese depart early from the far north, apparently beginning their autumn migration in late August so that by the first week in September they appear in staging areas of Saskatchewan and Alberta. When they leave these locations, the population splits. The majority are bound for California, but they will first pause in the Klamath Basin and the Sacramento Valley before arriving in December to winter in the San Joaquin Valley. Smaller numbers of Ross' geese winter in Texas, Louisiana, and New Mexico. During the fall migration and through the winter, these geese feed readily on rice, wheat, and barley when it is available. While foraging, they often mingle with snow geese and the small Canada cackling goose. Late in the winter, they feed on green grasses.

By early March the Ross' geese are on their way north, hopscotching along, trailing the fading winter. When the first week in June arrives in the arctic, so have the Ross' geese. Within a week they have selected a nest site, and the female deposits three or four white eggs and settles down for the three-week incubation period, during which she may lose as much as half of her body weight.

After the hatch, the entire family moves off to feed, and while the goslings grow quickly, the adult birds complete their molt. Forty days after they hatch, goslings are ready to take flight with their parents, only a few weeks before the migration begins.

Because the Ross' goose looks so much like the white phase snow goose, and because they often intermingle, it's difficult to accurately census these geese. For this reason, Ross' geese are included with snow geese in aerial wintering ground surveys and for the purpose of harvest management during hunting season. Trends over the last three decades seem to indicate a gradual growth in the population.

Emperor Goose

Called by some the most beautiful goose in the world, *Anser canagicus* is indeed a striking bird. Metallic blue-grey feathers on its back are edged with black and then with white, giving an irregularly banded appearance. A stark white head and neck with a dark front to the throat and chin all the way up to its pink bill set off the emperor's distinctive plumage. Immature emperors attain their white heads late in their first autumn, but are largely dark and unimpressive until then. With short wings and a heavy body, this six-pound goose flies low over the water with a rapid wing beat.

The emperor is largely an Alaskan goose, although a few breed in Siberia. It's also a goose that has figured out a way to avoid long migrations. Nesting mostly on the Yukon Delta of southwestern coastal Alaska, the 150,000 or more emperors simply fly a few hundred miles south in autumn to the Aleutian chain of islands, where they spread out for the winter, feeding on beds of eelgrass and sea lettuce in shallow ocean waters.

By the third week of September, the majority of emperor geese have arrived at Izembek Bay east of the Aleutians, where they remain for some time. As winter progresses, the population gradually works westward along the islands, continuing to feed until it's

North America's most beautiful goose, the emperor goose (*Anser canagicus*) is rarely seen because it never leaves Alaska.

time to reverse the migration. When the last week in May arrives, emperor geese are back at the Yukon Delta, selecting nesting sites on the edge of the coast. Most nest near tidal waters in loose colonies, choosing a site in grass, sedge, or tundra just beyond high tide. The goose lays four or five white eggs while the gander guards the site and grazes on grass and sedge. Because the climate here is a bit friendlier than the one faced by geese nesting in the arctic, emperor geese follow a less rigid schedule for laying and brooding, and have a very high nest success rate of nearly 90 percent.

The eggs take up to four weeks to hatch, during which time the non-breeding geese begin the molt. Parent emperors wait until three weeks after the hatch to wing-molt, completing the process in time to join their offspring's first flight. The geese will remain a family unit until late winter.

The Brants

Nesting on the coast of the Arctic Ocean as well as along its bays and seas, the brant is distributed across the polar regions of the northern hemisphere. Two races of brant are found in North America: the Atlantic brant, *Branta bernicla hrota*; and the black brant, *Branta bernicla nigricans*. Both are small geese of about three pounds, with short necks and small wings. Brant fly very near the

Taking a drink near this sleeping elephant seal, two black brant pause in California during their migration.

water's surface in long strings, often attaining speeds of over 60 miles per hour, making them the swiftest of geese. They have a remarkably soft, guttural voice, murmuring "r-r-r-ruk" or "ruk-ruk."

The black brant of the Pacific Flyway is, as its name implies, a dark goose that's deep brown on its breast and belly extending nearly back to its legs, with a brown back and black head, bill, neck, and chest. It has a whitish ring around its neck. The Atlantic brant is distinguished by its white belly and breast; otherwise, it's nearly identical to the black brant except that the white neck ring is not as pronounced.

At about 100 degrees west longitude,

in the Canadian arctic of the Northwest Territories, the breeding grounds of the two races overlap. The black brant nests along the coast and islands in this area west through Alaska to Siberia's Wrangel Island. The Atlantic brant nests from the common area east to the north of Hudson Bay and as far north and east as the polar-facing edge of Greenland—about as far north as the greater snow goose.

Black brant nest in greatest concentrations near the Yukon-Kuskokwim Delta. Atlantic brant nest on the many large and small islands of the east Arctic Ocean eastward to Greenland. Where their ranges coincide, some evidence of interbreeding exists.

What truly distinguishes the two brant are their wintering habits. The Atlantic brant migrates south through Hudson and James bays, eventually spending the winter along the Atlantic Coast from Massachusetts to South Carolina. Surprisingly, the largest wintering concentrations of Atlantic brant are found along the bustling coasts of New Jersey and in the bays of Long Island, New York. Some even cross the Atlantic after leaving their Greenland breeding grounds, wintering off of Ireland and England.

Black brant take a more circuitous route, following the Arctic Coast westward to the Bering Strait, then flying almost directly to California and, particularly, to the Baja and mainland Mexico. Fewer and fewer have chosen to winter off the U.S. coast in recent decades, the majority opting for balmy Mexico.

Both brant are true sea geese, feeding almost exclusively on eelgrass. This led to a serious decline in the Atlantic brant during the early 1930s, when eelgrass mysteriously disappeared along its Atlantic wintering grounds. Fortunately the Atlantic brant was able to switch to another food source, sea lettuce, and to grazing. After the switch was made, and thanks to the return of some eelgrass, the Atlantic brant made a strong comeback.

The black brant has not faced as severe a test, although eelgrass does occasionally become scarce in the Pacific. At such times it has also switched to other foods such as sea lettuce and has taken to grazing

The black brant is distinguished from its nearly identical relative, the Atlantic brant, by its dark breast and belly.

in meadows.

In late August or early September, black brant depart the breeding grounds for the Pacific, first gathering in huge numbers in the bay of Izembek National Wildlife Refuge on the Alaska Peninsula, where they feed on lush beds of eelgrass. From there they fly non-stop to the Baja, where they remain just a short while before beginning the return journey north.

Noted waterfowl researcher Frank Bellrose hypothesizes that the Atlantic brant fly almost non-stop from their most important autumn staging area on James Bay to the vicinity of New York City before dispersing along the Atlantic Coast. The majority of these geese will winter off the shores of New Jersey.

Most Atlantic brant begin their northward journey in April, arriving at their nesting grounds in early June. Some years, they must then wait for the snow to melt. Black brant follow the Pacific Coast more closely in the spring than they do in the fall, working their way back to Izembek Bay before completing the eastward leg of the migration. A few may even cross interior Alaska, a path not followed in the autumn. Both races have a strong homing instinct. Those that nest in the more westerly sites arrive in mid-May, while those flying further east do not reach home until early June.

Brant nest in colonies and arrive at the breeding ground in mated pairs. Both races choose low areas on small islets or tidal ponds and build nests in sedge. The nests are made of vegetative matter along with a large amount of down from the goose's breast.

Four or five white eggs are laid in the downy bed and incubated by the female for about 24 days. Males are very territorial during this period and, after the eggs have hatched, take over the work by leading the brood to open water and food. The young fledge in about 45 days. The adults molt

during this time, waiting until two weeks after the hatch before they begin. Most brant are able to fly by late August.

In recent years wintering Atlantic brant have totalled about 135,000. Black brant surveyed during the winter have shown nearly identical numbers.

Canada Goose

Branta canadensis is, for the majority of people in North America, the archetypal goose, the proto-goose. When the word "goose" is mentioned, this big, grey, black-headed, white chin-strapped goose comes immediately to mind.

Yet the "archetypal" goose may be anything but the original goose, for eleven races exist within the species, forming a grand spectrum of Canada geese distinguished primarily by their size and color. The species has evolved and adapted to be the most wide-ranging goose on our continent.

Currently, there are over three million Canada geese in North America, and their breeding range continues to expand to the south. This goose has also been transplanted to Sweden, Britain, and New Zealand.

Because they've adapted to the most ecological niches, it's likely that the races of Canada geese represent some of the "newest" geese, having split from a common ancestor some one million years ago. Canadas nest from the arctic south to the mid-latitude states; they breed on tundra, mountain lakes, prairie potholes, and urban ponds; they winter as far south as the Gulf of Mexico and north to Minnesota. The "ker-honk" of the Canada goose can be heard just about everywhere in the U.S. and Canada during some part of the year.

Classifying Canada geese can be a mind-boggling affair. Besides the 11 races, the geese are further divided into 12 populations comprised of up to four races each, primarily for purposes of management and hunting

regulations. The population designations are largely based on the composition of migrating or wintering flocks, and they reflect the propensity that Canada geese of various races have of mixing once they've left their respective breeding areas.

The 11 races of Canada goose are, from the largest in body size to the smallest:

Branta canadensis maxima,
or giant Canada goose;

Branta canadensis moffitti,
or western Canada goose;

Branta canadensis fulva,
or Vancouver Canada goose;

Branta canadensis occidentalis,
or dusky Canada goose;

Branta canadensis interior,
or interior Canada goose;

Branta canadensis canadensis,
or Atlantic Canada goose;

Branta canadensis parvipes,
or lesser Canada goose;

Branta canadensis taverneri,
or Taverner's Canada goose;

Branta canadensis leucopareia,
or Aleutian Canada goose;

Branta canadensis hutchinsii,
or Richardson's Canada goose; and

Branta canadensis minima,
or cackling Canada goose.

From east to west we can list the 12 populations of Canada geese and the races present within each population in descending order of numbers:

North Atlantic Population:
Atlantic Canada goose

Mid-Atlantic Population:
interior, Atlantic, and giant

Tennessee Valley Population:
interior, giant

Mississippi Valley Population:
interior, giant

Eastern Prairie Population:
interior, Richardson's, lesser, and giant

Western Prairie Population:
interior, giant, lesser, and Richardson's

Tallgrass Prairie Population:
Richardson's, lesser, and giant

Shortgrass Prairie Population:
lesser, Richardson's, and giant

Hi-Line Plains Population:
western, giant

Intermountain Population:
western

Northwest Coast Population:
dusky, Vancouver, cackling

Alaskan Population:
cackling, Taverner's, and Aleutian

The males of the largest of these geese, the giant Canada, weigh an average of 12-1/2 pounds. Some specimens approach 20 pounds. The tiniest of the Canadas, the cackling goose, weighs only about three pounds. Waterfowl scientists and managers further subdivide the races into the simple categories "large" and "small" Canada geese, although some races are so borderline in size that it's difficult to make clear distinctions. Small-bodied Canadas have shorter, heavier bills; larger races tend toward slender bills. It appears that the large- and small-bodied Canada geese began to split from a common ancestor about one million years ago; further splits within the two groups happened in the more recent past from 300,000 to 100,000 years ago.

Through recent advances in genetic studies, scientists have identified these separations by analyzing mitochondrial DNA, comparing genetic histories in the females of

LEFT: Very similar in appearance, the eleven races of Canada goose are distinguished mainly by body size and configuration.

the races. This is possible because a female goose (and duck) returns to the same nesting area each year, ensuring that its genes remain within its particular race, which stays within a fairly discreet nesting territory. She, in effect, carries the history of her race in her genes.

Because geese are clannish and return to the same nesting area in mated pairs, genetic information is passed slowly through the population. In other words, an adaptation made by Canada geese in Alaska is not likely to reach those geese that nest near Hudson Bay. Over many years, these small changes become characteristic of certain geographic populations, and eventually define a subspecies. Contrast this pattern to the mallard duck: While female mallards also have a strong homing instinct in nesting season, they choose new mates on the wintering grounds each year. A mallard drake that was hatched in Minnesota may very easily mate and travel north with a hen that hatched in Saskatchewan. The next year he may breed in North Dakota. His offspring will transport his genes to new regions. If the drake possesses some new and useful genetic adaptation, it is carried to a number of locations almost simultaneously. Thus there is much genetic uniformity amongst ducks, because adaptations are likely to spread through the population. The in-breeding of discreet populations of Canada geese creates just the opposite scenario.

The "large" races of Canada geese, in order of size, are the giant, western, Vancouver, dusky, interior, and Atlantic. The small races, also in descending order, are Taverner's, Aleutian, Richardson's, lesser, and cackling. The larger geese have proportionally longer necks and fly in generally smaller groups that are often made up exclusively of family members. Large Canadas have slower wing beats and a lower top speed. They also have a longer call that's issued in a lower pitch. Big geese call less frequently, often making appearances unheralded by their familiar honk. The "unk-unk" of the tiny cackling Canada is highest in pitch, and small races are much more vociferous than the bigger geese. Generally, the larger races nest in more southerly locations than the small races, which nest north and west of Hudson Bay through the arctic to Alaska.

No simple generalization can be made concerning color except that, no matter the size, the conformation among all Canada geese is quite similar. The sexes and ages, once reaching flight stage, are alike. The largest two races are lightest in color, but of the two darker Canadas one is the diminutive cackling goose and the other is the medium-sized dusky. Canadas breeding in western areas are customarily darker than their eastern relatives, and those indigenous to the coast of Alaska and British Columbia often sport white neck rings about an inch wide. Giant Canada geese quite frequently carry a white blaze on their forehead.

Canada geese, then, are all characterized by a generally brown-grey coloring on the back, wings, and sides, with a white belly, flank, and underside of the tail. The head, neck, and tail are black, and both ends are highlighted with white; the familiar chin strap appears on the head, and a white "V" shape separates the tail and rump. All Canada geese have black bills, legs, and feet.

Mating, nesting, brooding, and other behaviors are similar in all races of Canada geese; indeed, their behaviors are quite similar to those evident in other species of geese. Because the Canada goose is arguably the most-loved goose and is certainly the most numerous, the following chapters on behavior and migration will focus principally on this beautiful, admired bird.

RIGHT: The largest Canada goose, the giant, has the most serpentine neck. Males average 12 1/2 pounds—twice the size of the smaller races.

CHAPTER TWO

SO LITTLE TIME, SO MUCH TO DO

On The Nest

Wearily, the flock of Canada geese dropped from the sky, dark wings backpedaling in final descent. They came with an old gander leading, homing to their natal breeding grounds. The pale blue sky of this May day stood in stark contrast to the adverse weather the geese had fought on their way north as receding winter reluctantly loosened its grasp.

Broad Hudson Bay with its six-foot tides lay gleaming just to the north. As they came to their home, the geese looked down on the marshes of the bay's southwest; they saw vast, uneven stretches of muskeg, the plain dotted with irregular openings separated by hummocks of high ground. They had been searching for open water, but most of the openings were still stiff with ice, and the otherwise rusty high ground was still striped with bands of snow.

On a low, snow-free ridge strewn with rocky rubble, the geese landed on their black leather legs. Winds blew down from the arctic, and the birds shuffled and fed on the few withered grasses of the previous year, the breeze poking and lifting their feathers whenever they turned their backs to it. Tired, they waddled about. Their only tasks for now were to pick nest sites for the mated pairs and to wait for warmer winds. White flashing flocks of snow buntings swooped low over the muskeg, alighting to rest on their way to the arctic, picking nervously at plants for forgotten seeds.

The light snow cover and frozen ponds did not deter the geese much. They had encountered such conditions before, even in the area of southern Illinois where they had wintered, every time an arctic blast had reached south to numb the land. Even now,

in the cool winds, the tinkling rivulets running to join the black rivers that fill the bay were a sign of spring.

March in southern Illinois had been just warm enough to stir their instincts, and a day came when they knew they had to go, leaving the cornfields and cyprus lakes behind. Thousands had left before them, and many would stay south even longer.

The departing geese knew the difference between warm and cold, the distinction between frozen and wet, but they didn't know they had followed north what humans call the 35-degree isotherm, which marks the thawing of the land. They knew that the warming rays of the sun unearthed foods—grasses and clovers, wasted grains in farm fields missed by mechanical pickers. They knew, too, that open waters meant drink and rest, and only when they flew too far and too fast did they realize their mistake. They were caught in late winter blasts over frozen lands and waters and forced to temporarily retreat.

This flight north, unlike the autumn migration, came in short hops of ten, fifty, and one hundred miles, only as far north as open water and food prevailed, paced by spring's inevitable progress.

Across a grand panorama they had flown: over broad, black, earthen farm fields; over the glaring lights of restless cities; above the open, frigid waters of Lake Superior; and over black spruce forests dotted with lakes and laced with frothing rivers. Flying at heights of up to 3,000 feet on clear days, they wended their way north in a group of a dozen goose families, joining tens of thousands of other geese for a few weeks in Wisconsin's Horicon Marsh.

All across North America, other geese of all types were in one manner or another

LEFT: With only a few short months to produce a family, all geese are busy in summer.

preparing for, facing, or completing a similar journey. Some giant Canada geese—those that call the mid-latitude states home—needed only to travel a short distance to nest. But others of this giant race were flying farther north, almost as far north as the smaller Canadas, to the prairie and parklands of Manitoba. Some Canadas flew from the rice fields of Texas, but mostly it was lesser snow geese that were being heard in the skies of the southern plains.

In the rainwater basins of south-central Nebraska, tens of thousands of white-fronted geese mixed with thousands of Canadas and hundreds of thousands of lesser snows, feeding constantly in the red smartweed marshes and damp grain fields, building reserves for the arduous nesting season.

Brant on both coasts were feeling the urge, flying from bay to bay, north and north, resting on estuaries ripe with eelgrass. Canada geese also surged along the continent's two coasts, and greater snow geese fled to Quebec, the migrators a blizzard of white pausing on the St. Lawrence River. To Alaska, to Ellesmere Island, to the mainland Canadian arctic, millions of geese faced their yearning in skies filled with the promise of spring, echoing their honking cacophony.

The Snow Goose: Dressed For Success

While the mid-continental population of snow geese (those that migrate through the Mississippi Flyway and the eastern part of the Central Flyway) consists of between 25 and 50 percent blue phase birds, those that migrate down the Pacific Flyway are almost exclusively white phase. In addition, geese with the plumage coloration and patterning of both phases are not rare.

Why two colors? Why does the same goose come dressed in varying versions? It may be dressed for success.

Snow geese nest in the far north, in colonies containing up to 200,000 nests with as many as 3,000 nests per square mile. Some birds will be white, others blue. Because of the northerly breeding grounds, these geese must initiate nesting early enough to raise a brood before the short summer ends. Snow geese may have evolved two color phases to deal with the unpredictable nature of arctic summers and to better ensure nesting success.

For instance, when spring is late with snow still covering the ground, the white birds are naturally camouflaged. White phase geese initiate nesting before the blue phase in any year, and although nest failure due to predation is higher for the white birds during a normal season, they appear to be more successful when the arctic summer is short, because they have gotten a head start on rearing a brood.

If the breeding season begins with a mild spring and the nesting grounds are free of snow when the geese return, the blue geese suffer lower predation rates than the white, probably because they are now the better-camouflaged phase. Thus, whether or not there is snow cover on the breeding grounds, some snow geese will always be dressed for success.

The two color phases are generally segregated on both the wintering and nesting grounds, but mixed mated pairs do exist. A factor lowering the likelihood of mixing is that of "imprinting." Hatchlings of blue parents are also blue, and white begets white. When young, the hatchlings imprint on their parents' color. Because they have imprinted on birds of their own color, they are inclined to select mates of the same color when they reach breeding age, perpetuating the process.

Most geese nest near water and line their nests with down plucked from the female's breast.

During these first few days on the south of Hudson Bay the mated pairs, led by the smaller females, began their search for nest sites, breaking away from the rest of the flock and even from offspring of the year before. They searched diligently for a spot, the right spot, black heads craning, dark eyes sweeping the maze of ponds and points, examining in slow flights each tiny muskeg island. Each carried a personal or ancestral picture in its mind of what this nest site would look like, the older geese miraculously finding amidst the jumbled tundra a spot they had used in years past and younger geese relying on molecular memory to reveal a proper place.

Canada geese seek to nest in the same marsh year after year, conditions permitting, and they even use nest scrapes from previous seasons. The experienced pairs had been mated now for a number of years and were on familiar ground. Though they had selected each other after long association during their first two years of life, most did not mate and reproduce for the first time until they were three years old, a trait they share with most other geese. Only when habitat is uncrowded and weather conditions are optimal will geese attempt a breeding in their second year. Even then, they fail more often than the older birds to produce a brood, perhaps because of a lack of experience and possibly because the

best nesting sites—and therefore the best habitat—are taken by the more seasoned geese.

There was an urgency to their search. They had arrived in the north in condition to begin nest-building and egg-laying. The females were fertile and wanted to drop eggs. Mating had taken place while pausing to rest along the way on the recently opened waters. Since the day the pairs had chosen each other—the choice often dictated by a battle between two ganders hissing for the favors of a particular goose—they had flown in pairs.

On the flight north they stayed near each other until, resting on chilled April waters, each gander had approached its

goose by swimming at her side, dipping its long neck under the water as if bathing. Soon their mates responded and pairs dipped in unison, throwing cold water over their backs. Finally the ritual led to copulation, the gander climbing onto the back of his mate, gripping her neck feathers in his bill. When they were finished, pairs arched their breasts upward and out, pointing necks and bills straight to the sky, exchanging calls.

Canada geese nesting in the far north seem to know the summer is short, with much to do. The smaller races that nest farthest north, as well as the lesser snows, Ross' and brant that nest along the arctic coast and islands, have proportionally less time to nest and raise a family.

Rub-a-dub-dub, Goose in a Tub

Canada geese are quite willing to accept unusual nesting islands of many types, especially if you define "island" as a spot isolated from predators. On cliffs overlooking the Missouri River, giant Canadas nest 200 feet above water and encourage their goslings to take leaps of faith to the ground when only days old. Explorers Lewis and Clark reported in 1805 that they found Canada geese nesting in cottonwood trees along western riverbanks. The birds still do that today, often usurping the nests of ravens, owls, herons, or osprey. When wildlife managers sought to reintroduce geese in areas from which the birds had been extirpated, they found that many of the marshes did not contain enough (or any) of the small islands Canada geese prefer; and many were located in regions containing large numbers of predators. Consequently the managers tried nesting structures of all types. Because these man-made sites were largely predator-proof, the geese experienced high reproductive success. Which means, of course, that their young would also seek and accept similar devices.

Washtubs elevated up to 20 feet above the water on posts have been accepted by Canada geese, as have dirt nesting islands, elevated wire and wicker baskets, and floating platforms. Imagine a majestic Canada goose sitting in a washtub atop a post!

On the Copper River Delta in Alaska's Chugach National Forest, the U.S. Forest Service, in cooperation with Ducks Unlimited, has created over 800 artificial nesting islands of various types, to increase the nesting success of the troubled dusky Canada goose population. Those geese nesting on the artificial islands enjoy an average 70 percent success rate, compared to a 26 percent average for those nesting on shore and facing severe predation.

LEFT: Young geese learn to fly and adults molt to replace worn flight feathers during the brief summer season.

Though rituals and habits differ, all geese form strong and customarily lifelong pair bonds.

This flock of the interior race of Canadas, part of the Mississippi Valley Population, nested near the southwest coast of Hudson Bay, only a few miles from the eastern edge of the Eastern Prairie Population's range and from colonies of lesser snow geese. The marshes, which had been still and silent, suspended by winter, erupted in life as geese and birds of many kinds swept in to nest or rest, and the sun began to warm the land. The breeding geese were ripe with the urge to nest. Daily their low flights over the rusty archipelago of marshy islands continued, until each searching pair homed in on its nesting site.

Youth deferred to age. Older pairs claiming sites they had used before re-established their territory, an area that was for the most part respected by other mated pairs. When the boundary wasn't honored, it was defended fiercely.

Though Canada geese use a wider range of nest sites than other waterfowl, most sites share similar traits. This colony's sites were typical of the nesting spots of all races of Canada geese. They offered enough cover for the nest itself, but the cover wasn't so dense that it obscured vision. They were located slightly above, but near, the water. And food could be found nearby.

Whenever possible, the geese chose nest sites atop small islands on miniature

Copulation usually takes place during the spring migration, so that the female is ready to reproduce when she arrives at the nesting ground.

muskeg pothole lakes—spots that would offer some protection from predators. Canada geese across the continent, from Kentucky to the Kuskokwim Delta, choose such islets—even ones as small as a muskrat house or a haystack surrounded by flooding. Some Canada geese elsewhere, especially those in areas marked by more human impact, take to nesting in man-made structures such as aerial baskets elevated above a marsh, or on floating platforms.

Wherever they nested, Canada geese fought to control a certain area around them, territories as spacious as conditions allowed. Instinctively they knew that the larger the territory, the more successful they

would be, for nest abandonment occurs if goose pairs must compete.

While the pairs had been searching for nesting sites, more waves of Canada geese poured in from the south. Though some had left wintering areas weeks after the earliest migrants, most arrived within days of each other. Those leaving late made up for lost time by flying much greater distances each day. A few warm days had passed and the land had begun to thaw, snow melting into the spongy turf and the waterways flowing. Days of sun encouraged the turf to eat the remaining snow, and the ice on the marsh had first turned to black then suddenly disappeared, issuing boggy sounds. By the time

the majority of the ponds were ice-free, the anxious pairs were on their nests.

Most pairs prepared to lay their eggs in old nests, mere hollowed scrapes in the earth, females pulling vegetation into the hollow from nearby, arranging it in a bowl about four inches deep and a foot wide inside. Because Canada geese vary so widely in size and habitat, nest size and composition are also quite variable. Giant Canadas make giant nests, often of matted bulrushes, that are twice the size of the spongy delta nests used by the tiny cackling goose. Like other waterfowl, Canada females add down to the nests, plucking it from their own breasts after laying most of their eggs.

When the construction of the nests was nearly completed, the geese began to deposit eggs at the rate of one per day until most had a clutch of five. Each morning, and again late in the evening, the females would leave the nest briefly to feed, drink, and preen. This was their only break from sitting on the eggs, and each goose was attended by her gander. Since each female had her own routine and schedule, the marsh was constantly in motion.

Geese popped up and down in their nests, turning their eggs over. Every 50 minutes the female stood up, rotated the eggs with her bill, then pushed them together again with her feet as she settled down. Throughout the incubation, geese reached out from their nests to add small bits of material, keeping the nest from getting matted flat. Though the eggs were pure white in the beginning, they were soon stained a ruddy color from the vegetation of the nest. A warm drift of down surrounded them.

The Canada geese were nesting earlier than other waterfowl—indeed, earlier than almost all other birds. While the ganders guarded the nests and the females incubated, clouds of snow geese passed above in the watery blue sky, on their way to a huge colony on the McConnell River delta and even farther north.

One evening a spring storm blew in from the northwest. Dark skirts of clouds dragged on the horizon and with them came driving snow, forcing the geese to huddle tightly over the eggs while their mates stood nearby, helpless but attentive. When the whipping winds had finished and morning's unheralded light returned, a blanket of snow was draped across the marsh, covering even the geese in their nests. The well-insulated birds shrugged off the matted snow and waited for the sun to reappear.

Though geese outnumbered the other birds in the area, they certainly weren't alone. Amidst the geese, beneath clumps of brush, willow ptarmigans huddled over their own eggs. Grouse-like birds with perfectly dappled summer camouflage of brown, black, and white, the ptarmigans, unlike the geese, were nearly invisible as they sat in their nests. The males, obvious in their yet-unchanged, winter-white bodies and their contrasting rusty necks, could occasionally be seen strutting and feeding on the short, spongy turf, eyed by northern harrier hawks that floated above them.

Above the constant sound of gently lapping waters, and punctuating the sporadic grunting of the geese, the mournful "ooo-ooo" of the sleek, black-and-white-checked male arctic loon was heard daily as he swam and fed, his grey mate crouched on a hidden nest somewhere in the marsh

As the days warmed, the Canada geese sat dutifully atop their nests. Salt breezes blew in from the coast; fields of flowers brightened the short summer. June was in full swing now, and the sun barely dipped beneath the horizon before it rose again. The electric "whrrt-whrtt" of neighboring nesting sandhill cranes charged the air, while geese mothers waited along with eider ducks, surf scoters (sea ducks) and yellowleg sandpipers

LEFT: Female geese, unlike female ducks, receive support and protection from their mates during nesting and brooding.

for the hatching of eggs. Clouds of black flies and mosquitoes tormented every warm-blooded creature, reaching even the geese through their thick feathers.

While the females sat, the ganders stood guard. Canada geese are adept at defending their nests because of the strong pair bond, and because of the gander's aggressive nature. Still, all across their range, they or their eggs fell prey to predators. In the north, arctic foxes harassed geese from the nest, then devoured the eggs. To the south, the red fox behaved similarly. Occasionally a female, weakened by the stress of incubation and left alone while her mate was feeding, was killed and dragged off to be eaten by a silvery arctic fox.

In the agricultural regions of the Canada's nesting range, red fox, skunks, and raccoons raised particular havoc. Though geese and small, egg-eating predators have been natural enemies for eons, man has altered the more southerly landscape to such a degree that the predators abound—in numbers far beyond what is natural. These areas, devoid of large predators such as wolves that would maintain the predator balance, and with modified habitat that has benefited and expanded the range of small predators, make nesting nearly impossible for many species of ducks and other ground-nesting birds. Nesting is difficult even for Canada geese.

Near Hudson Bay, the nesting geese were also harassed by the parasitic jaeger, a dark seabird that resembles a cross between a hawk and a gull, which took time off from the haranguing of gulls to swoop ferociously down upon the geese. Ganders repeatedly rushed out in defense, as they do with any predator or intruder, hissing and rearing up at the jaeger. For some of the geese, the hooked bill of the jaeger was too terrible. A few were driven from the nest. The fierce bird quickly dived in, breaking the eggs open and consuming the contents.

Predation is the major cause of nest failure from year to year, but adverse weather can have a broader effect over a short period. Nearly half of the nests that fail are lost to

Best in The Nest

Geese are among the most successful of wild parents. Their strong pair bonds and fearless defense of their young lead to high reproductive rates, no matter the goose species.

Adverse weather and predators are the two most significant causes of nesting failure.

In most Canada goose races, 48 percent of losses can be attributed to predators. Desertion of nests, which can be caused by numerous factors, accounts for 42 percent of the failures. Because Canadas nest very near water, nine percent of the failures are caused by flooding. The failure rates for other species of geese are not as closely studied, but are likely to be quite similar.

Despite the losses, Canada geese reproduce successfully about 70 percent of the time and, starting with an average of five eggs per nest, rear an average of 2.8 goslings per pair up to their departure for autumn migration. Atlantic and black brant also have a 70 percent success rate, rearing 2.3 goslings per pair. White-fronted geese enjoy an 85 percent success rate, duplicating themselves at a rate of 3.4 goslings per pair. But the nesting champs seem to be the Ross', lesser snow, and emperor geese, all of which can be successful as much as 90 percent of the time.

During incubation, female geese rotate their eggs about once an hour to ensure even distribution of warmth.

predators. Almost as many nests are lost due to desertion, which can be caused by either predators or adverse weather conditions. Because green grasses near a nest site are critical to success, late snows and freezing weather can limit the amount of food available to the geese. When this happens early in the breeding season and relief is slow in coming, the female may reabsorb the eggs instead of laying them. If such conditions persist for a long period over a wide range, whole populations of geese may not even attempt to nest.

Once the clutch has been laid, similarly poor weather may cause the geese to depart in order to survive, or can actually result in starvation for the female while on the nest. In either case, the eggs are lost. When ducks face poor nesting conditions, they may leave and attempt to nest in other areas. They will re-nest up to three times in one year if their first attempts are unsuccessful. Geese, though adaptable in many ways, are less flexible in this regard and will simply abort the nesting process. If a female loses her gander during incubation, nest abandonment is also common, for she is undefended against aggressive pairs or predators.

Here, the weather had been moderating slowly, and the geese enjoyed the long days. The last snow dropped by the spring storm had melted, enlarging the muskeg potholes.

Some nervous females watched as water lapped nearer their nests, but it stopped inches or feet away. In some years many nests are flooded; flooding is a smaller but still significant source of nest failure.

Those geese who had small islands to themselves were faring the best. Others that had nested too near to one another on larger islands were stressed by the constant competition; some chose to abandon their eggs rather than facing repeated threats from more aggressive pairs. Those that chose to leave their eggs may have been younger pairs more easily intimidated. Whenever choice habitat is crowded, older geese invariably out-compete their younger counterparts. Goose populations made up of many juvenile birds reproduce poorly compared to those comprised largely of experienced geese.

Despite the first week's snowstorm, despite the jaegers and prowling foxes, and despite some quarreling over territories, the Canada geese had largely settled down for the remaining three-week wait. The marsh was now full of the sound of grunting mated pairs and the hissing of ganders as they rushed intruders. Over the rattling of winds in the willows, the clucking ptarmigans could be heard; the geese turned watchful eyes to the sky when the "pee, pee, pee" of the northern harrier overhead froze them in their tracks. But if everything went well during the next three weeks, the marsh would fill with the sound of peeping goslings.

Far Trek: The Nest Generation

Canada geese have an amazing ability to adapt to areas where no goose has gone before. Consequently, these flexible fliers can be found nesting across North America from coast to coast and from Florida to the arctic islands. Each race of Canada goose has adapted to its nesting grounds. Most refrain from intermingling, which helps maintain the genetic distinction between the races.

Small Canadas nest farthest north, from the western range of the Aleutian goose on the outermost islands of the same name east across the sub-arctic east to Baffin Island. Richardson's, Taverner's and lesser Canadas comprise the bulk of these northern breeders.

The larger Canada geese nest for the most part south of 60 degrees north latitude. The Atlantic race is found in Quebec and is densest along the east coast of Hudson Bay. The southwest coast of Hudson Bay, from James Bay west to Churchill, sees the bulk of nesting interior Canada geese, although many nest across Canada on the myriad lakes of northern Manitoba and Saskatchewan.

Canada geese of the Western race breed from central Saskatchewan and Alberta down through the western states, south as far as northern California and Utah—wherever basins containing both water and grazing can be found. Dusky Canadas breed on the Alaskan southeast coast for 140 miles in either direction from their central nesting grounds on the Copper River delta. The Vancouver race nests from that area south to Vancouver Island along the coast of British Columbia.

The giant Canada nests wherever it pleases, but primarily in scattered small populations throughout the prairie states and provinces, and in the mid-latitude states from coast to coast. Many giant Canadas are barely migratory. They comprise the bulk of the urban geese we're becoming accustomed to seeing.

Geese enjoy higher nesting success rates than ducks. The larger, pair-bonded geese are more effective nest defenders.

Old Feathers, New Feathers

Most of the colony members had laid their eggs by early June. Now, four weeks later, there was a scurry of activity. The peak of the short summer had arrived, and with it came the year's goslings, each breaking free of its egg with the aid of its pointed egg tooth. Eggs of a single nest generally hatched within a day, and the goose kept the tiny, yellow fluffballs in the nest with her through the first night, sometimes covering her brood with a protective wing to fend off the cold and wind.

All over the marsh the sound of peeping arose as the goslings experienced their first days. The tundra was stitched with strings of waddling geese as parents led the broods from their nest, some beginning as soon as the goslings were dry, others waiting for up to a day. In every case, the procession was the same: Beneath the wan sun, a female led a tumbling, yellow parade while the gander stood guard at the rear, fending off other geese and predators.

The ganders guarded with good reason, for while the summer is a lush time of varied foods and growth for the geese, it is the same for those creatures that feed upon flesh. With the sudden appearance of thousands of defenseless, downy young, the marsh served as a surging supermarket for predators and, for the patient ones, it represented an

opportunity to feed their own restless infants.

These first few weeks of life would be by far the most dangerous for the geese, and the greatest risk would occur when families took their first walk after hatching. But that first walk is unavoidable; the move to water and feed is critical for both the young and the parents. The goslings must reach flight in just eight or nine short weeks, and the parents need to restore the vigor lost during the arduous nesting period.

The small size of the goslings—they're about seven ounces at birth—and the general confusion took its toll. Goslings were struck down by jaegers or snatched by foxes. In warmer climates elsewhere, small geese were even devoured by large fish or turtles during their first swim.

Birds of Few Feathers Flock Together

For three to four weeks each summer, geese of all species undergo the molting process, shedding old feathers and growing new ones. While this transformation takes place, they are flightless.

The yearlings molt first, followed quickly by the two-year-olds and any older birds that aren't paired or nesting. Generally this takes place while the breeding pairs are just beginning to nest. In many cases the geese molt on the edge of the breeding grounds, congregating in large numbers for protection. Native peoples in both Canada and Alaska continue their age-old practice of herding and killing some of these flightless geese for food.

Several races of Canada geese undertake a molt migration--an unusual phenomenon that takes tens of thousands of non-breeding geese far from their nesting areas. Groups of mixed races of Canadas gather in the Thelon River area 200 to 300 miles west of Hudson Bay to undergo their molt. The majority of these geese are of the large western and giant races that have flown 1,000 to 2,000 miles north of their breeding areas. In some years thousands of interior Canadas, which normally nest south and west of Hudson Bay, over-fly the Bay to molt on the Ungava Peninsula of Quebec, the breeding region of the Atlantic race of Canada geese.

Although these migrations have evidently been taking place for many years, a rather more recent phenomenon has been documented. Canada geese from several southern flocks in Minnesota, Ohio, Illinois, Wisconsin, and nearby states are now winging their way to coastal James and Hudson bays to molt. These spring flights of non-breeding geese are the result of dramatic population increases in resident U.S. flocks. Waterfowl managers are concerned about how these molt migrations may affect the geese that normally nest in these areas, especially regarding competition for food.

There is no doubt that geese leaving the nesting grounds of their race to molt in other areas reduces the amount of competition for food needed by the breeding pairs and their broods. However, little is yet known about the effect the molt migrations have on areas where other races nest. It's interesting to ponder what stirs these geese to fly thousands of miles north to begin with. How do they find their way, when many are yearlings with little experience and are members of races that never otherwise migrate so far north?

LEFT: Tiny, seven-ounce goslings find life a challenge from the moment of birth. They face wind, rain, long marches to water, and danger from predators.

Within a day of hatching, goslings are led to water.

Because they were nesting on shallow tundra potholes, most of these geese did not have far to lead their broods. They guided their young to the pothole's edge, mere yards from the nest. Those nesting near the great bay took their peeping broods on a perilous journey to the coastal marshes, a walk of nearly five miles for some. In other parts of the Canada's range, this first journey sometimes stretches for many miles, and whole families often drift down streams to areas with better food. Others move miles from inland to tidal marshes. But wherever they first meet water the goslings, without hesitation as their mothers gently call, enter for a first brief swim, floating amazingly high in the water.

During the summer days, the goslings were taught to feed on aquatic plants, although their buoyancy made it difficult for them to tip butt-up and head-down like their parents and in the manner of ducks. On land, things were different. With legs located nearer to the center of their body than most ducks and swans, the geese easily moved across the flatlands—a characteristic that distinguishes them from most other waterfowl. They milled about, grazing like so many cows on the tender green grass. Their serrated bills, tipped with a sharp cutting edge, made clipping the vegetation easy, and the bill's sensitive tip helped them readily

RIGHT: As the first three weeks pass, gosling down gradually turns grey. Feathers begin to appear at about four weeks.

This goose's wonderful wings will be rendered useless for flight during its annual three-week molt. During this period, worn flight feathers are replaced.

find and pick up seeds. Feeding was almost constant, up to 18 hours a day, a response to the need to grow large enough to make the autumn migration, which now loomed so near in the future. For a short while longer the females continued to brood their young, gathering them to their warm, protective breast at times of sleep. Gradually this behavior ceased, though the goslings still sometimes slept in a jumbled pile of yellow siblings, guarded by their parents.

After weeks of preparing for and taking care of the year's brood, the mated pairs were now ready to take care of some business of their own. The goslings, now three and four weeks old, were sprouting their first

feathers amidst their greying down. Wing feathers were visible and tail coverts took form. Their parents were also experiencing a change in plumage. They had begun their wing molt, replacing worn flight feathers.

The breeders, however, were not the first of the colony's geese to replace their worn feathers. The immature, unmated geese had left the breeding grounds earlier to flock together. Some molting geese moved only a few miles from the breeding grounds. But many more of the youngsters and pairs that had not bred continued north hundreds of miles to experience their molt, starting while the mated pairs were still on the nest. They left the breeding area to the new families,

LEFT: Geese that are unmated due to youth or loss of a previous mate leave the nesting colony to feed elsewhere.

OVERLEAF: The long northern days provide growing geese with necessary feeding time. They may feed for up to 18 hours per day.

reducing the competition there for food.

The molting parents, bedraggled and unable to fly, tried to keep their exploring goslings from trouble in secluded parts of the breeding marsh. In some places families gathered in large groups, finding safety in numbers. Despite their inability to fly, the parents remained determined defenders, running swiftly toward intruders and using their wings to deliver stunning blows to any creature foolish enough to attack their young. The goslings continued to develop. They learned which foods tasted good, and they stretched and flapped their developing wings, rushing ten feet across the water's surface, feeling their first intimation of flight.

When five weeks had passed since the majority of the goslings hatched, the brief, lush subarctic summer was already half over. The goslings looked more like geese. They had lost down and gained grey feathers, and their white chin straps were evident. When eight weeks had passed, they looked almost like mature geese, nearly fully feathered. All across the marsh, young geese stretched their wings in mock flight, determined to fly. The parents neared the completion of their molt only days before the entire family would be ready to take wing.

An uneasiness came to the marsh. Cold days spit snow. September came, and so did those geese who'd flown north to molt, returning to the marsh to rejoin families. Groups of geese took wing more frequently; they swung round and round the marsh, calling. Some did not return, their voices drifting to the south. Swooping waves of shorebirds came and went.

The families of geese fed constantly. The goslings now weighed almost as much as their parents and could fly nearly as well. Family joined family. Like a great army readying to march, they assembled in ordered confusion. Mate honked to mate, and parents honked to broods; thousands and thousands honked, and wild cries filled the marsh with anticipation. When the lead ganders could stay no longer, their flocks suddenly rushed into the sky on pounding wings, lifted by favorable winds.

The great, grey, honking autumn migration of Canada geese had begun.

The Goose: Adult or Juvenile? (Number of feathers reduced for clarity)

JUVENILE TAIL
Note notch at the tip of each tail feather

ADULT TAIL
Note dark feathers with no notches

TAIL IN MOLT

JUVENILE WING
Note pointed, worn primary feathers

ADULT WING
Note rounded, dark primary feathers

RIGHT: As the short summer ends, adults and juveniles are ready for the long autumn migration.

CHAPTER THREE

SOUTHBOUND

Great Goose Gatherings

The motel bed faced the dresser. On the dresser sat a slightly slanted mirror. The slanted mirror faced a western window. And I lay back on the bed, facing the ubiquitous motel TV and awaiting the evening news.

Rascal, my black labrador retriever, went rigid where she lay on the floor, ears at attention. I looked at her, then back to the TV, my eyes passing over the mirror. Then I went rigid.

In the mirror were thousands of geese. Snow geese. A white undulating ribbon of snows, miraculously appearing on one edge of the mirror and vanishing as they flew out its end. Confused for a second, I stared. Then it dawned on me.

I ran to the window, and the dog came with me. The grey North Dakota sky was alive with geese, flying from where they had fed that day to where they would roost for the night on the waters of nearby J. Clark Salyer National Wildlife Refuge. I cranked open the window to hear the parade; goose gossip flowed into the room through the portal. The dog jumped up, planting her front feet on the window sill. We stood transfixed.

There seemed no end to the flock. I threw on my jacket, clipped the leash to the dog's collar, ran down the hall and out the door, and stepped into the cold October dusk. The geese still came. We walked, watching them.

The tiny town in which we were staying petered out just a block from the motel, engulfed by a sea of wheat stubble. Rascal and I stood in the midst of one field as a cool wind and thousands of geese swept around us. Finally the flock thinned and dwindled, until late stragglers, their bellies full of wheat, squawked by in search of their cohorts. The

sun sank into the prairie. In the darkness we could hear the last geese pass, hear the barking honks, hear the sweeping pinions.

• • •

I don't know if I could live in a world devoid of the sight and sound of migrating geese. I suppose I could. I *do* know I wouldn't want to, and I suspect there are many like myself.

There are those who love the presence of geese, the wildness they entail, the mystery of their coming. There are those who are thrilled to watch the geese move, to see them slip air and come to water, to see them mill about in grainfields. There are those who love to hunt them. These passions are not mutually exclusive. I know. I love all these things.

When we see geese migrating, something ancient in us stirs. An ancient human stands with us, marvelling in an unknowing way, wondering from where these geese have come, where they're going, if they portend anything beyond the approach of winter, if perhaps some message is written in their wavy flight. Our "ancient self" senses the melancholy that comes with the approach of winter, feels the need to prepare and the sadness of saying good-bye to summer. The world is chilling down, freezing up. Food and warmth loom as critical concerns. We're envious, for we can't go where the geese are going; we can't fly to warmth. We're hungry, and we envision geese in our winter larder. An older, cleaner, larger, more primal world flashes through our collective memory, vanishing when the geese vanish.

Like some mysteries of faith, we accept migration without fully understanding it.

LEFT: Gathering in large flocks in staging areas, geese are hounded by impending winter.

And, even understanding parts of it, we remain amazed. The migration of wildlife, especially the highly visible flights of geese across entire continents, astonish us. We get lost going across town. We need detailed road maps to find Aunt Sophie's place down state. Sextant and compass, satellites and computers—these are the tools we need to cross the distances commonly navigated by geese. And so, rightly and humbly, we marvel at their abilities.

If we contrast our own tools to those of the geese, we're at first struck by the complexity of ours and the simplicity of theirs. At first. But think about it. A magnetized needle floating in an enclosed vessel of alcohol is hardly complicated. But the tools of the goose are.

Think of the structure of their eyes. We couldn't make them.

Think of the intricacies of the racial and individual memories that map their migration, that comprise their traditions. We couldn't learn them.

Think of the delicate yet surprisingly strong structure of their wings and feathers. We can't emulate them.

Somehow, some way, geese have mastered skills that we can learn only with much difficulty. And no endeavor of geese epitomizes this mastery more than their cross-continental journeys—their great gatherings.

Most species of geese gather in late August or early September to prepare for their migration. While some depart in rather small bunches comprised of family groups, especially the largest races of Canada geese, most congregate in large masses within regions central to the breeding grounds. This move to "staging areas" comprises the first leg of the migration, and from these locations the large flocks we witness are launched.

To understand *how* geese migrate, we must first ask why. The obvious answer is that they're fleeing winter, fleeing the certain death that would result from wintering in the arctic. But how do they know winter is coming? How do they know where to go with such precision that the same flocks winter in the same place year after year? How do young geese, making their first migration, find their way to the wintering grounds of their race, even when separated from the flock and its leaders?

It's not happenstance that geese locate prime resting and feeding areas half a continent distant. Their survival depends on it. Whereas a migrating songbird need only find food and the shelter of just about any kind of dense cover, geese must find water large enough for safe roosting and fields of grains or greens on which to graze. They do this with an accuracy born of necessity. Just as there is an ancient human standing with us when we watch the geese, so there is an ancient goose within each bird, complete with its memory of the ages.

Some scientists theorize that waterfowl migrations evolved gradually after the ice-age periods. Imagine a time when the northern hemisphere was nearly covered in glaciers. We (humans) were wearing skins, following migrating mammals, and working the edges of the herds to kill stragglers, much like our competitors, the wolves.

As did all creatures, ancient geese lived south of the glaciers, in regions of warmer weather and abundant water and food. But the years flowed, the weather warmed, the ages passed, and the glaciers retreated ever northward, leaving in their wake bits and pieces of themselves in the form of landlocked melting icebergs, shallow glacial lakes, and flowing meltwater.

Eventually, marshlands sprung up in these wet areas as vegetation pioneered north, seeds and spores borne on the winds. Waterfowl, including geese, began to make use of these marshes, perhaps spreading

RIGHT: The secrets of migration are locked within the mind and molecules of each goose.

gradually as regions to the south became crowded, finding in these marshlands uncrowded habitats in which to breed and feed.

Still, the winters were cold in the north. Geese could not survive when the marshes froze and snow covered the grasslands and tundra, limiting all foods. Short migrations must have evolved from the then-nearer "arctic" to the ancestral marshes. With each successive generation the distance from north to south increased, but from each generation was passed the knowledge of how to find the way to warmer winters, and so today geese routinely navigate from the arctic to the latitudes of Mexico. Theirs is a tradition of migration stored at a molecular level, or so the theory of the beginning of migration goes.

Others disagree. No one knows for sure. But I'll admit that I like the idea of geese pushing ever north in the wake of receding glaciers and the notion of our ancestors, busy hunting mastodon, eyeing the geese curiously. And no matter how the migrations evolved, it's certain that the knowledge needed for such long flights is at least partially instinctive, a legacy of past generations.

And so the geese gather each autumn (actually, they gather in what's late summer to you and me) to repeat this tradition. Some species, like the white-fronted and Ross' goose, depart early, appearing in staging areas about the first of September. Others seem to taunt the early arctic winter, delaying departure until mid-September. In most species, departure is preceded by a

Geese gather in family groups in late summer and early autumn. Then the families join others for migration.

gathering of families and the non-breeding birds that had molted elsewhere, all assembling in the general region of their racial nesting grounds.

What exactly triggers these gatherings and the onset of migration is still largely unknown. Weather is most certainly a factor for some, yet geese will often remain until roosting waters freeze and snow covers their food—while others of the same species and geographic region depart much earlier. Scientists infer that geese leaving before conditions force their departure are really responding to some kind of internal clock, one programmed over the eons to stir departure before the birds can be caught by adverse weather.

Those geese adhering to this unknown schedule are responding to physiological changes that may be triggered by the ratio of day to night, known as the "photoperiod." The light changes affect the pituitary gland of the bird, stimulating the release of hormones that control the cycle of its entire year. We can certainly empathize with the geese for, as we all know, hormones can spur all kinds of amazing behavior.

Geese that remain behind for a longer time aren't refusing to respond to hormonal urges, but may simply be delayed by some concrete need. Perhaps they were late arrivals on the nesting grounds, due to poor weather. They may have produced a late-maturing brood, and may be staying to allow the goslings to mature and their own molt to be completed. Geese that suffered through harsh weather while nesting may need to restore lost vigor and weight, feeding until

The change in the length of day, known as the photoperiod, stirs the goose's hormones and triggers migration impulses.

Migration requires great exertion. Geese burn their stored fat reserves and stop to feed as they make their way southward.

the last possible moment before undertaking the rigors of migration.

All migrating birds need to store reserves of fat for the flight, and those geese whose fat levels aren't sufficiently high probably linger north because they "don't much feel like leaving," just as humans might unconsciously postpone tasks for which they're unprepared. Females lose considerable weight during the nesting period—often up to 25 percent of their body weight. Recent research indicates that a late hatch due to poor weather or overpopulation on the breeding grounds can lead to large numbers of growth-retarded goslings. Such goslings have less time to feed before departure and

must compete with other, stronger geese for short supplies of food. Some evidence indicates that these late-maturing, low-weight geese never do catch up in size with better-nurtured cohorts, and they may be less productive breeders when their time comes. Some may never breed at all.

The importance of fat reserves is easily understood when we consider just how much energy it takes to fly the great distances involved in migration. The black brant that nest in the central Canadian arctic spend winter off the coast of the Baja. Just the first leg of their journey requires a flight west along the entire coast of the Arctic Ocean—for some a distance of more than 1,000 miles. These small geese then pause for over a month on the north side of the Alaska Peninsula, to feed on lush beds of eelgrass in Izembek Bay.

Having already flown half the width of a continent, the brant will continue on a non-stop flight of 3,000 miles over the Pacific before coming to rest off Mexico. During that last three-day leg of their journey, as they maintain a continuous 50 miles-per-hour speed over open stretches of the Pacific, they'll burn a third of their own weight—the one pound of fat added at Izembek Bay.

While some geese will undertake the entire migration in small flocks, or even as a single family, most will migrate in the company of many others, meeting at specific staging areas. Think of these spots as focal points to which members of the same species funnel and at which they prepare for migration. They add critical stores of energy in the form of fat, just as the gathering of brant does on Izembek Bay. These staging locations, especially on the mid-continent prairies, may serve a number of races of Canada geese or even a number of goose species. Staging areas, whether during the autumn or spring journeys, differ from migration areas. Though concentrations of geese may be similar in the two types of rest spots, geese remain much longer in staging areas, building fat. Migration habitats generally serve for shorter rests.

Canada geese of the interior race that nest on the southwest coast of Hudson Bay depart in small bunches, and may not return to earth until they reach Horicon Marsh in Wisconsin, 850 miles to the south, where they'll be joined by thousands of other geese in a month-long wait for winter before heading to southern Illinois. While such a distance seems impressive, contrast this journey with the travels of the greater snow goose. Greater snows flee Greenland and Ellesmere Island before the end of August and won't gather until they reach the St. Lawrence River below Quebec City—three times the distance flown by the Hudson Bay geese, and half a continent to the south from their frigid nesting area.

As various species leave the north, the flocks remain segregated by species, but where their migrations overlap, they often share resting and feeding areas. In other words, while there may be a large number of both Canada and snow geese in the same vicinity, the snow geese will fly out together and feed together, and the Canada geese will do the same. Though the wheat fields in which they browse may be next door to each other, the species generally do not intermingle.

Behavior is much the same on roosting waters which, in these migration rest areas, are largely government-owned refuges amidst an increasingly developed world. Canada geese, large and small, are often seen flying or feeding together in flocks of mixed races, especially as they near the wintering areas where the "funnel" narrows and suitable habitat becomes scarce. Except for sea geese like the brant, feeding flights take them to privately owned property, primarily in farm fields that have replaced the native meadows and prairies.

And so the migration begins, with geese responding to the chimes of some unknown clock, each species gathering family by family on the staging areas, then passing to the south, resting and feeding, keeping just ahead of winter.

Geese: Center Stage

Like performers beginning a play, geese gather at center stage to begin their annual production—fall migration. Their staging areas are historic, used year after year unless the sites are affected by drought or other adverse conditions.

The spectacular gatherings that take place at these important migration areas are well worth seeking for those who wish to see large concentrations of geese. Some of the most important sites are as follows:

White-fronted geese

Departing Alaska, 200,000 whitefronts fly 2,000 miles to the Klamath Basin in northern California, gathering in late October and early November.

Mid-continent white-fronted geese stage near Kindersley, Saskatchewan. Populations peak here during the last week of September. Another group stops on the Souris River in North Dakota during the first week of October.

Lesser Snow Geese

Easterly populations stage in a huge gathering at the south end of James Bay, the most southerly extension of Hudson Bay, in early October. Those using the most easterly migration corridors (through Wisconsin, Michigan, and Illinois) fly non-stop 1,500 miles to Louisiana.

In early through mid-October, other eastern arctic populations swing down corridors further to the west (Minnesota and the Dakotas), stopping in large numbers on Whitewater Lake in Manitoba; on the Souris River refuges in North Dakota; and on Sand Lake National Wildlife Refuge in South Dakota.

Lesser snows of the western arctic stage on the MacKenzie River Delta in the Northwest Territories, passing through to pause in numerous southeastern Alberta and southwestern Saskatchewan resting and feeding areas before heading west toward California.

Greater Snow Geese

These eastern arctic geese migrate through Quebec, and the entire population gathers on the St. Lawrence River some 40 miles downstream from Quebec City. Some geese arrive in mid-September, but the bulk of the population arrives in October. During the last half of November the flock departs for wintering areas.

Ross' Geese

Ross' geese stage on northern Alberta's Athabasca River delta in September, then migrate south and west, making many of the same migration stops as the western arctic lesser snows.

The Brants

Atlantic brant stage on James Bay in mid-September and early October, then fly overland to wintering areas along the coast of New York and New Jersey.

As many as 250,000 black brant gather in September and October at Izembek National Wildlife Refuge near the tip of the Alaska Peninsula.

Canada Geese

Canada geese populations fan widely across North America during the autumn migration. Each group uses dozens of national wildlife refuges and other places to gather and rest along the way. In addition, local populations of breeding geese exist through much of the U.S., and these geese make short migrations to areas where they join the northern birds.

Some important gathering places are, from west to east: Bristol and Izembek Bays, Alaska; Klamath Basin, California; Hanna, Alberta; Kindersley and Quill Lakes, Saskatchewan; Whitewater Lake and Oak Hammock Marsh, Manitoba; most North Dakota, South Dakota, and Minnesota national wildlife refuges; Silver Lake, Minnesota; Horicon Marsh, Wisconsin; Shiawassee National Wildlife Refuge, Michigan; Lake St. Clair and Jack Miner Bird Sanctuary, Ontario.

The most easterly races often refrain from gathering in large numbers until they're in the area where they will winter.

Resting spots popular with geese must offer water (for drinking and roosting) and nearby food sources.

The Power of Flight, the Mastery of Navigation

Responding reluctantly to an urgent call of nature, I put on a warm jacket and stepped from the camper into the cold, dark Manitoba night. Black Rascal vanished once out the door.

A nearly full moon threw twisted shadows to the oak forest floor as light streamed through the branches. Bright stars fairly shined. It was cold, and the little lake nearby was rimmed in ice. The colder it is the brighter the stars, and these were very, very bright.

I stood beneath the heavens, waiting for Rascal to return. From the west the call of snow geese came faintly, and I held my breath to better listen. They were coming our way. As I strained to see them in the night sky, Rascal loped up and sat beside me, ears up, listening too.

High in the nearly cloudless sky the snow geese flew, heading south by southeast, passing directly above. They were maybe 2,000 or 3,000 feet up. There were two, or maybe three, dozen geese.

We watched as they passed by, losing sight of them long before our hearing failed, then returned to the warm camper. As I lay back in the bunk, deep in the sleeping bag with a snoring labrador curled at my side, I wondered how far the geese had come this night and how far they would yet go. And even more, I wondered how they found their way in a dark October sky.

Though we may be able to feel some sense of *why* geese migrate, *how* they do it is quite another matter. They possess two magnificent abilities—the power of flight and the mastery of navigation.

Flight is probably the ability we envy most. I would forsake the skill needed to pilot myself across great distances if told that I would be able to revel only in the glory of flight. Bound as we are by gravity, we fly only in our dreams.

But geese must also obey the law of gravity; they've been given no special dispensation. However, they've developed their own "legal loopholes." Dependent as they are on aquatic environments, which can dry up or freeze over, geese must travel, and creatures that can fly are the most efficient travelers.

Flight is a magnificent tool of survival, one that enables geese to exploit different types of habitats at different times of the year. By spending spring and summer in the far north, they can nest across broad areas relatively free of competition. Since we know that competition is a major cause of nest abandonment, we know that solitary summers increase survival rates.

Wintering in the south, though a more social gathering, reduces encounters with harsh weather and food shortages. Even in day-to-day life, flight means that geese can exploit a diverse range of habitats—fields for grazing, moist-soil marshes for feeding, and open waters for roosting. And of course, flight is a wonderful escape mechanism when threatened by predators.

We need only give geese a cursory glance to see how efficiently they're built for flight. With tapered faces and long necks, with sloping chests and streamlined bodies, and with wings contoured to thin leading edges, the entire goose has evolved toward flying efficiency. The wings are broad and arched to produce lift; as air flows over the top of the arched wing it's compressed, though the air beneath the wing is not. Since the constricted air passing over the curved top of the wing travels faster than the air below, a difference in air pressure is created. Because the pressure is lower on top, the wings are lifted and the goose's body, swinging pendulum-like between the outstretched wings, is lifted with them. And so geese exploit the first loophole in the law

LEFT: Built for long-distance flight and equipped with exceptional navigational tools, geese routinely cross continents.

of gravity.

Beyond the broad, central section of the wing is the first wing joint, or wrist. From this joint out to the tapered tip of the wing, along the rear edge, are the feathers known as primaries. On most species of geese, the primary feathers are various shades of grey, blending into the coverts (which shape wing profile) on the upper front of the wing, and the secondaries (smooth for aiding lift), located along the central rear of the wing.

If you've seen the shiny black feathers on the wing tips of a mature snow goose, you'll quickly recognize the primaries, for they are most distinct in this species. These are the critical feathers that, if missing as they are during the molting process, render the goose flightless. These ten feathers are responsible for providing thrust. They are also the same amazingly strong, light feathers that were treasured by Native Americans for use in fletching arrows. Considering that there are some 20,000 feathers on a goose,

cunningly layered like overlapping shingles for protection and providing a smooth surface that minimizes drag, it seems difficult to believe that the loss of ten primaries will ground such a flying machine.

But a goose doesn't fly just by hanging in a stiff wind and allowing lift to form beneath its wings. Those primary feathers develop forward thrust during the down stroke, provided the wrist is rotated forward. As a secondary air flow created by the down stroke streams over the wings, forward wing rotation "lifts" the goose forward; it's not pushing against anything, nor is it scooping air. So the second loophole in the law of gravity employed by the geese is the ability to thrust themselves along by creating lift.

Fueled by fat reserves and propelled by wings, geese do not cross those great distances without effort. Their broad wings are powered by the strong pectoral muscles of their breast—muscles that comprise 30 or more percent of the goose's weight. Have

Fussy With Feathers

During the autumn migration, part of the molting process continues as body feathers are replaced. As fall rolls toward winter, new body feathers make young geese less distinguishable from their parents. By winter they're virtually identical to adults.

However, with a bird in hand, it's relatively easy to tell a juvenile (under a year old) from an adult. During fall and into early winter, geese less than a year old will have notches in the ends of their tail feathers. These indicate spots where the early feathers of down broke off when tail feathers first emerged.

Once these feathers have been replaced through molting, age is more accurately determined by examining the primaries nearest the wing tip. Juvenile geese will have pointed primaries; primaries on adult birds are rounded.

Since each goose is the keeper of 20,000 feathers, there's a lot of grooming to be done. A portion of every day is spent grooming—combing and oiling feathers. At the base of its tail, each goose has a preen gland, from which it extracts an oily substance made of fat and wax. Collecting this oil on its bill, the bird rubs the compound on its plumage to keep the feathers smooth and water-repellent. By rubbing its head on the preen gland, a goose is able to spread oil on areas it can't reach with its bill. The oil also keeps feathers from fraying and wearing prematurely.

A goose's broad breast is comprised of dark muscles rich in oxgen-storing compounds.

you wondered why the breast meat of a goose, duck, or woodcock is dark red, nearly purple? Have you wondered why the same meat on a chicken, pheasant, or ruffed grouse is white? If you have, you've inadvertently stumbled on the reason geese can fly such great distances, whereas a grouse can fly only for short hops. You've also discovered the reason for the marked difference in taste.

A ruffed grouse's white meat is delicate and delectable. It's also high in carbohydrates. Carbohydrates are great fuel; they burn rapidly, powering grouse to their thundering flushes. But a slower-burning fuel is needed for continent-hopping. Waterfowl depend on stored fat, which metabolizes more slowly but is more fuel-efficient because it contains twice the energy of a comparable amount of carbohydrates. The value of the fuel is enhanced by the goose's efficient and remarkably rapid digestive system, which processes a diet of grasses and grains into the fat needed for fuel.

The phrase "loose as a goose" doesn't describe moral behavior, but how rapidly geese expel wastes from their system while proficiently building fat reserves. The red, arguably more robust-tasting breast muscles of a goose effectively utilize this fat fuel because they contain compounds that store the oxygen necessary to metabolize fats. What all this means is that those wonderful

Geese can simultaneously see above, below, and to each side.
They often use landscape clues and celestial bodies for navigation.

feathers atop those powerful wings are being propelled by a slowly turning, fuel-efficient engine that's perfectly designed to cover great distances without rest.

But none of this explains how geese manage to fly so accurately—that is, how it's possible for them to unerringly navigate tremendous distances.

When Canada geese, for instance, depart the shores of Hudson Bay, the first leg of their journey takes them across vast tracts of spruce and pine forest. Whether they're part of the Eastern Prairie Population bound for the Dakotas or members of the Mississippi Valley Population scheduled to arrive at Horicon Marsh, they're faced with a task that requires precision. A slight error in navigation could put them in hostile surroundings without food or roosting water. No doubt a few geese over the ages have made such mistakes, invariably succumbing to the errors and eliminating their genes from the population.

The geese that navigate best find rest and food more easily. Consequently, they are also less stressed, survive more often to reproduce, and pass along their genetic and learned skills to their offspring. In such a manner, migratory accuracy becomes racial memory.

Waterfowl have more than one tool available to them for navigation. The most obvious is their excellent vision, used to spot landmarks and landscape cues along the way. They also use vision to keep an eye on the heavens, by which geese seem to be able to practice celestial navigation. But when flying on cloudy days or nights, or in the midst of storms and fog, vision becomes less useful, perhaps even useless. Mounting evidence indicates that birds contain an internal compass, by which they can navigate.

The eyes of a goose are located on the sides of its head, providing primarily monocular vision; its binocular vision, the kind humans possess, barely extends to the tip of its bill. Monocular vision lacks depth perception, but the goose's eye placement more than compensates by giving the bird the ability to see simultaneously almost completely above and around itself—a tremendous advantage in spotting predators and one that provides a panoramic view of the world and stars for use in navigation.

Although geese have acute hearing, eyesight is probably their most important sense—which makes sense, when you think about what flying would be like with anything less than superb vision. Geese see color in addition to seeing great distances, which explains why a hunter stands no chance of bagging a goose unless he or she is well-camouflaged and perfectly motionless.

When geese migrate they use large landscape features to guide them. But these are not their sole visual guides. Apparently, geese are able to use the relative position of the sun and stars as aids to navigation. How they do so is not yet understood, but numerous controlled experiments with birds and a wealth of field observations by researchers seem to indicate that geese do indeed make use of celestial navigation.

As you and I would most likely use landmarks to triangulate our position, a goose, able to see nearly all around itself, could be collating information from landmarks below with its orientation to the stars above, constantly adjusting its aerial path.

How many among us have stood listening on a foggy morning, the still dampness mysteriously pierced by an ever-increasing clamor of honking geese? How many of us have heard them pass so near we feel that we

Geese can navigate accurately even through fog and clouds, possibly by using iron-rich tissues in their brains that respond much like the needle of a compass to the earth's magnetic field.

could have reached up to touch them with a pole? How many have stood spellbound as their music drifted away, enveloped in the mists?

In such a fog, I could have determined which way was north with my trusty pocket compass. But geese have no pockets, and they have no compass. Or do they? We're quite certain they lack pockets, but we're less certain about the compass. Waterfowl routinely migrate in weather that obscures the visible clues of heaven and earth. Scientists probing the mystery of bird migration report one startling find: the presence of a small quantity of iron-rich tissue in the brains of some birds—tissue that responds to a magnetic field in much the same manner as a compass.

In tests, homing pigeons were unable to find their way home when released near iron deposits emitting a magnetic field; yet the same birds easily found their way when released outside the range of this natural magnet. Though studies to determine whether geese have the same internal magnet have not been done, it seems likely that they, along with other migrating birds, are gifted with the same tool as the pigeon.

In concert, all of these amazing tools allow geese to routinely cover vast distances with pinpoint accuracy. And though all species of geese may have the same skills, they may not use them to the same degree, because particular migrations place particular demands upon them. Lesser snow geese seem to utilize landscape cues less extensively than the easterly populations of Canada geese. Because the earth's surface yields fewer navigational cues for the lesser snow geese migrating over the relatively featureless plains, they probably navigate primarily by referencing the sun and the stars.

Eastern races of Canada geese benefit from highly visible landscape cues, such as the Great Lakes and numerous large river systems, by which they can guide themselves. Of course, their methods aren't foolproof. All species of geese occasionally get lost in bad weather or are blown off course by fierce winds, but even in these instances they seem to realize they're lost. After regrouping, they backtrack or otherwise make adjustments, eventually finding their way to traditional migration stops or wintering areas.

Geese often fly no farther than they absolutely must. The Vancouver race of Canada geese is barely migratory, often traveling less than 100 miles to spend the winter. Similarly, the emperor goose migrates only a short distance from its breeding grounds on the Yukon Delta to the Aleutian Islands, where it gradually moves west over a period of months. Many flocks of giant Canadas in the mid-latitude states, and some as far north as Minnesota, simply refuse to move on, even in sub-zero weather, as long as food and water are available. Those that avoid the migration benefit by being the first to "return" to nesting sites and to secure their territories.

At times, this non-migration is not a natural phenomenon. Some Canada geese persist in the north largely because they're aided by humankind. Food is available now that was not historically present, either in the form of feed intentionally supplied or in waste grain scrounged from farm fields. Humankind has also provided critical winter roosting water by building huge reservoirs that are too large to freeze completely, or by keeping rivers and lakes open with warm water discharges from power plants and sewage treatment facilities. If rest, food, and water are available, many geese are predisposed to make the most of a good thing by staying rather than migrating.

Geese will migrate both day and night. Some species, like snow geese, actually prefer night departures when beginning their treks. Whenever possible, flocks will

RIGHT: Arriving before nightfall, these geese may be preceding a storm that drove them from a location farther north.

The familiar "V" formation aids on long flights by providing air currents that help geese lift their weary wings.

take advantage of favorable winds; many among us have seen geese arrive on strong winds that precede the storms that have driven them south. In many instances, geese will wait for a storm driven by a low pressure system to cease, since a high pressure cold front normally follows behind, providing a strong wind from the northwest to carry them on their way.

Many species of geese maintain a 50 miles-per-hour speed for long periods during migration, although a goose might slow to a mere 20 miles-per-hour when cruising in search of food or rest. Generally, the larger the species of goose (or race of Canada), the slower their flight and wing beat.

Consequently, the tiny brants are the fastest of our geese, hitting speeds of up to 60 miles-per-hour.

The formations in which geese fly serve to aid their speed. Both species of brant often migrate in trailing lines. The birds frequently change order, skimming the ocean at an altitude of just 20 feet. The emperor goose also flies in such a configuration, although at a slower speed and with changes of position in line occurring less frequently. Like bicycle racers, these geese are employing a technique known as "drafting." The forward goose breaks up the air, creating a back draft that sucks the rearward goose along and minimizes drag.

All other species fly at higher altitudes and employ a slightly different technique—the familiar V-formation or its variant, the check-mark. Both the Canada and white-fronted goose appear to be the most adept at flying in fluid V-formation. Snow geese utilize the formation as well, but with much more shifting. Individual snows frequently rise and fall above the plane of the "V," giving the flock an undulating appearance that accounts for their colloquial name of "wavie."

Snow geese also have a greater tendency to fly in an offset line, a formation that resembles a check-mark. When brant fly in a string, the air flow is broken for the birds following. But when Canada geese use the V-formation, they gain the advantage of lift. As air spills off the tips of the forward goose's wings, it helps power the next goose's upstroke, saving it energy. Another advantage of either the V or check-mark formation is that each bird has an unobstructed view.

Formations serve another purpose—they reduce stress and allow geese to fly much farther in flocks than they could as individuals. In small family groups, the oldest gander usually leads the flock, especially on feeding flights. But when large flocks of mixed families travel together in long migrations, the lead position changes often.

On a blue-sky autumn day, as we stand in our yard raking leaves, we sometimes hear Canada geese honking but are unable to spot them. More than likely, these geese are flying so high that we can detect them only after a careful search. How high might they be? Canada geese generally migrate at a height of about 2,000 feet when weather permits. However, they've been spotted by pilots or on radar at altitudes of up to 8,000 feet. Both lesser and greater snow geese migrate at slightly higher average elevation—near 3,000 feet. Some lesser snows fly at elevations of up to 12,000 feet. Whatever the elevation, geese choose it not for the scenery but to find a favorable wind, one that will make their passage easier.

Autumn progresses. Winds are howling in the arctic, baring their teeth to the south. Driven by those winds and by urges even stronger, the geese trickle in families,

This pair will soon lead its family far to the south.

Funnels of Flight

Many of us have heard of the four waterfowl flyways: the Pacific, the Central, the Mississippi, and the Atlantic. Actually, ducks and geese pay very little attention to these designations, for the flyways were set up for people, not for waterfowl.

Flyway Councils set up in 1948 offered wildlife managers a means of organizing, a way of sharing information, and the ability to establish hunting regulations based on a rough geographic approximation—functions the councils continue to perform today. But except in a few instances, waterfowl do not spend their entire lives in just one of the flyways.

A more accurate picture of the actual migration route is the concept of "migration corridors," first proposed and researched by noted waterfowl biologist Frank C. Bellrose of the Illinois Natural History Survey. Although geese are more likely to stay within the north-south vision of a flyway than are the more wander-prone ducks, many goose species do travel laterally, a characteristic taken into account by corridors. The corridors are much narrower than flyways, and they tend to become more restrictive the further south they extend, much like the tapering of a funnel.

Migration corridors have been documented by using radar to register actual goose flight paths. By compiling an enormous amount of radar data and using information from hundreds of pilots who were asked to report any waterfowl migrations they observed, Bellrose was able to map the corridors.

Further information about the shape of corridors comes from leg banding studies. In these studies, geese are live-trapped on the breeding grounds and fitted with an aluminum leg band. The band contains coded information that registers the location and date of the goose's capture. When the leg band is later retrieved, usually by a hunter who has bagged the goose along the migration route or near a wintering area, the location of the recovery helps delineate the migration pattern of the goose.

In addition, banding has helped determine which populations of Canada geese nest and winter in particular locations. For example, though the Mississippi Valley Population nests very near to the Eastern Prairie Population, they winter separately, and each population is named for the location where its geese spend the winter.

Survival rates of ages and sexes, as well as mortality from hunting and natural causes, are determined through banding studies. Anyone who retrieves a goose with a leg band should mail the band to: Bird Banding Laboratory, Laurel, MD 20708, unless another agency's address is visible on the band.

Migration corridors lead geese to familiar winter resting areas.

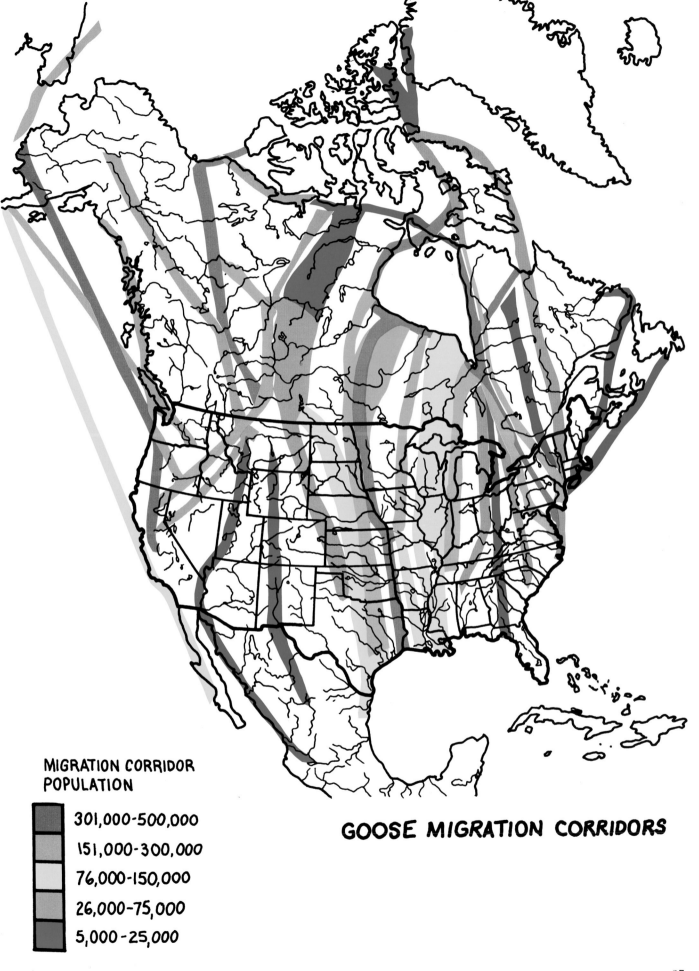

MIGRATION CORRIDOR
POPULATION

301,000-500,000

151,000-300,000

76,000-150,000

26,000-75,000

5,000-25,000

GOOSE MIGRATION CORRIDORS

87

flowing en masse, passing through the heart of a continent and down the wave-tossed coasts. Guided by memory and tradition, gifted with flight and a mastery of navigation, migrating geese appear in our changing world, adapting age-old behaviors to fit the needs of the human race. And with their migration, we witness an indomitable spirit.

Winter Rest

When they reach the Canadian prairies, geese enter a world that has drastically changed in the last century. Perhaps those birds riding the winds of both coasts notice the change farther south than do the birds of the Central and Mississippi flyways, for development in the northern forested regions lags behind development on the easily manipulated prairies. But no matter where the goose originated, it will in just a few short days leave a mostly natural world for one that's highly manipulated.

Development has caused great changes in migration behavior. To understand, we must realize that a goose's autumn and winter behavior centers around eating, resting, and attempting to maintain good physical condition—all in an effort to ensure better odds for reproduction. Their entire yearly cycle is geared toward the climax of summer and the production of a brood. So they fly south to areas with good weather and lush foods.

Traditionally, most geese wintered far to the south of where they do today. Wintering areas were marshes, and the foods were moist soil and aquatic plants as well as native grasses in fields and meadows. Only in the south, or in northerly micro-climates warmed by ocean influence, could geese historically find green grasses and marsh plants as well as open water during the winter. But as we will detail in the next chapter, humankind has both purposefully and accidentally changed goose behavior by providing new sources of food and roosting waters.

Additionally, geese are much sought by hunters, and the majority of hunting takes place in goose wintering ranges. Hunting has changed the way geese behave and altered the locations where they're found through disruptions in traditional patterns. Unregulated hunting early in the century drove some goose populations to record lows, and in the face of high mortality some geese sought new areas in which to roost. There is some evidence that the races of Canada geese wintering in the deep south were more heavily hunted than those farther north. Since geese are so bound by traditions based on survival rates, populations that were over-shot diminished, while those that found safety elsewhere prospered.

Because of strict regulation and sound wildlife management, today's hunter poses little threat to the overall health of the goose population. Modern goose hunting serves as a management tool to control goose populations, but it both accidentally and purposefully affects wintering behavior. It's also a type of recreation that, for some hunters, borders on religion. In some areas of the country, goose hunting is a major industry, infusing millions of dollars into rural economies. The economic results of hunting play a role in goose management and, therefore, in goose behavior.

Human manipulation and hunting pressure do not change the goose's primal need to prepare for the mating season—they only change the way in which this is done. Geese still make their daily feeding flights, though they fly now to fields of corn and rice instead of grazing grasslands or smartweed marshes. They may fly higher to avoid the hunter's guns, merely demonstrating the same wariness they would use in avoiding any other predator.

Despite the changed locations, winter remains mostly a question of consumption for geese, and their routines remain centered

WRANGEL
ISLAND

SELAWIK

ARCTIC
SLOPE

SEWARD
YUKON
DELTA

OLD CROW
FLATS

ICELAND

GREENLAND

BANKS ISLAND

KOYUKUK

KANUTI

MACKENZIE
DELTA

BYLOT
ISLAND

INNOKO

KUSKOKWIM

YUKON
FLATS

VICTORIA
ISLAND

BAFFIN
ISLAND

SUSITNA

TANANA

ANDERSON
RIVER
DELTA

KENAI

NELCHINA

QUEEN MAUD
GULF

BOOTHIA
PENINSULA

BRISTOL
BAY

COPPER
RIVER
DELTA

CHESTERFIELD
INLET

UNGAVA
PENINSULA

SOUTHAMPTON
ISLAND

SLAVE RIVER
PARKLANDS

McCONNEL RIVER

CHURCHILL

CAPE HENRIETTA
MARIA

ATHABASKA
DELTA

CHILCOTIN
PLATEAU

CARIBOO
PLATEAU

SASKATCHEWAN
DELTA

PUGET
SOUND

INTERMOUNTAIN
REGION

DELTA
MARSH

COLUMBIA
BASIN

MALHEUR
BASIN

GREAT LAKES
CONIFER REGION

KLAMATH
BASIN

CARSON
SINK

CHESAPEAKE
BAY

CENTRAL
VALLEY

GREAT SALT
LAKE MARSHES

NEBRASKA
SANDHILLS

CURRITUCK
SOUND

IMPERIAL
VALLEY

= IMPORTANT FLYWAY
& WINTER HABITAT

= IMPORTANT BREEDING AREAS

IMPORTANT BREEDING
AND WINTER HABITATS

Although they're built to withstand cold, geese may choose to rest
and forego feeding on frigid days. It's a strategy that helps them save energy.

on roosting and feeding. Each morning and afternoon, geese leave the sanctuary of refuge waters to fly to nearby grain fields or pastures—flights that are often influenced by weather and light.

Geese are not generally early risers like their duck relatives. They dally a while in the morning, rather than leaving the sanctuary of roosting water at first light. An anxiety seems to build in the marsh as the morning passes. A few geese sound off with anxious honks, joined soon by others. Perhaps they're waiting for enough light to see by, but at some point near 8 a.m.—a point determined by no particular goose—the flocks begin to lift in groups until the roosting area is suddenly empty of geese.

Morning flights are often delayed on cloudy days, and the flights may even be forsaken in extreme cold weather. If the temperature drops below 10 degrees Fahrenheit, the amount of energy expended on feeding is greater than the intake, so the geese remain at roost. With their feet pulled into their flank feathers and their bills tucked beneath the feathers of their backs, geese conserve warmth and energy during cold spells and can go for nearly a month without feeding. Large races of Canada geese have a lower surface area to body weight ratio, and can withstand cold weather more easily than their smaller cousins. Hence the

As long as open water and food uncovered by snow remain, geese easily tolerate cold weather.

larger geese winter within the snow belt, while small races depart for the south.

Sometimes geese feed at night, under the brightness of a full moon. Though flocks may be feeding in fields miles apart, it's not unusual to see all the geese cease their feeding and return to water at nearly the same time, as if on a predetermined schedule.

Feeding flights during the winter can take on enormous proportions, as thousands of geese lift almost simultaneously from the roost in search of food. These large flocks are an adaptation of the "safety in numbers" rule. Large flocks are much less susceptible to hunters, for they will rarely come to decoys. Geese have a tendency to stay together until

they reach the fields in which they feed. And once on land, large flocks can feed safely and efficiently, using a strategy similar to the one employed by herding mammals.

In order to eat, a goose (or bison) must lower its head to the ground. This makes watching for predators difficult. A goose feeding by itself would need to spend a great deal of time watching its surroundings for danger, giving it less time to eat. And geese must eat a lot. Due to the relatively low quality of their forage, they require hours of uninterrupted grazing. In a large group, there are many eyes and ears to alert the congregation to danger, allowing each member to feed more and watch less.

OVERLEAF: About mid-morning, wintering geese gather and fly out to fields in which they can feed.

Geese will return day after day, until they've gleaned the last waste grain of wheat from a field or have grazed pastures down to the ground more efficiently even than sheep. As the weeks and months pass, the feeders may need to fly as far as 15 miles from the roosting area, a feat that barely seems to trouble a bird that crosses continents.

There's another important concern for wintering Canada geese as spring nears. Now is the time for young Canadas to form their pair bonds. Since those bonds generally last a lifetime unless a mate dies, and because that lifetime can be very long (up to 24 years for Canadas), geese have reason to take the selection process seriously.

Pair bonding is not quite the same as mating courtship, which customarily occurs in the older pairs during the flight north in the spring. Mating courtship occurs each year, each time a couple decides to breed, whereas pair bonding represents the decision to become a couple, often culminating in first copulation. Unlike Canada geese, snow geese and Ross' geese apparently form their pair bonds on the breeding grounds.

Using blunt black bills and broad grey wings as weapons, male Canada geese sometimes fight over a female during the pair bonding process. The victor approaches the female with his head held low, weaving his neck from side to side. If she deems him "worthy," she will accept his attention and the pair bond will become a permanent one.

Those geese that have survived the rigors of migration, the dangers of the hunting season, and the risk of disease begin to feel the coming of spring in the February air. All species of geese feed intensely as they prepare for another migration. But stores of fat are now important for another reason.

For the fall flight, fat served as fuel. But spring conditioning is even more critical, as the fats and proteins consumed now will determine the number and viability of eggs and, ultimately, the survival of the brood. The hormonal clock that instigated the flight south is now ticking toward another journey.

Migration. Winter. The long miles of flight from the north, the long months of feeding and survival. Daily flights to nearby fields. Roosting nights in refuges and on reservoirs. Months of hunting pressure from Canada to the Gulf.

In a changed world, geese manage to do all that their tradition requires. But they no longer do it on their own. Despite the wildness that they represent, geese must fit into the niches we've left them. They must now meet our demands.

We've altered their patterns. We sometimes find ourselves in conflict with their behavior. We've encouraged some geese to trade their wildness for popcorn in parks. Although they inspire us, they've also become a crop, a nuisance, a competitor. Though they're wild during their spring and summer stay in the north, they're managed and manipulated in the winter. Goose management is not just a science in which we indulge. As we shall see, it has also become a necessity.

RIGHT: Winter is a period of resting and feeding for all species of geese.

CHAPTER FOUR

OF GEESE AND MEN

Dark-barked cypress trees stood buttressed against the water. Mallard drakes with iridescent green heads swam among the trees, cruising slowly through the flooded forest. In the recesses of the swamp, ice had formed during the night—a smooth skin of winter prevailed wherever the sun had not probed.

Rascal and I walked along a narrow road. Cardinals, flitting red in the late morning light, startled us. Occasionally a mallard hen strained her vocal chords in a raucous quack, alerting or berating some other of her kind. Bright as the morning was, the southern Illinois air was crisp; much colder, the locals told me, than was normal for early December.

It was so cold that the evening before we'd been forced into our camper, which shook in the wind, gusts of snow rapping pellet-like against its side. The accumulation amounted to two inches or more by morning, causing much consternation in a region unaccustomed to such weather. Huddled inside the camper, we had warmed up after watching thousands of Canada geese arrive in the gale, watching as they dropped wearily from the white evening sky, watching as they twisted like storm-tossed leaves falling into the shallow ponds of Union County Refuge.

As the geese left Union County Refuge to feed, we departed on the white morning, driving south to see the South, driving south to see more geese. It was nearing noon before we paused at a cyprus swamp to watch the mallards swim in the waters of Horseshoe Lake Refuge, an ancient land-locked, oxbow bend of the Mississippi River.

I had never seen a cyprus tree before. I had never seen ducks swimming in a forest. But these things I expected to see in my three-month journey following the flight of waterfowl from Saskatchewan to Louisiana. I had not, however, expected to see what happened next.

Heralded by their voices, Canada geese swung high in the pale blue sky over the cyprus forest, and I craned my neck to watch them. Like airplanes in holding patterns above a busy terminal, bunches of geese circled in turn, waiting to descend. One by one, as if given clearance to land, the flocks spiraled toward the water.

I have seen geese come spraddle-legged to a wheat field, hitting the ground at a dead run. I have seen them swoop to a lake, black-leather webbing spread, skiing to a stop. But these geese came like none I had ever seen, approaching the cyprus-studded lake at a low angle, wings set on glide, only to suddenly flip onto their sides or flop completely over onto their backs, spilling air from beneath their wings, dropping in a controlled plummet through the branches of trees, down, down, and onto the frigid water. Each one was a stone. Each one, no matter how it twisted, kept its head atop its serpentine neck oriented to the water. And near the end of this finely executed plunge, each quickly cupped more air, lowered its wide landing gear, and hissed onto the water.

I stood dumbfounded. I had seen ducks and geese turn over like this before—a technique for controlled descent called whiffling, in which they emptied their feathered sails of wind. But what I had never imagined in a million years is that these great grey geese could corkscrew down through timber, twisting through the branches. I was duly impressed.

For 45 minutes Rascal and I watched. Some were big geese, perhaps giant Canadas.

LEFT: Humans have changed the landscape. We have also greatly changed the lives of geese.

Geese have adapted to both urban and rural environs.

Others were much more compact, with shorter, thicker necks—Canadas of a smaller race. All executed the same maneuver, and the clamor of the happy geese on the water increased, ceasing shortly after the last flock had come to rest. The far shore shone from silver stretching wings and flashed with white undertails, as geese tipped beneath the water.

Barring unusually inclement weather, these geese had probably flown as far south as they would go. They would be content to spend the winter on this little lake, feeding daily in Illinois corn fields. Geese that had nested on tundra and had winged above broad Hudson Bay now settled in for a two-

or three-month winter wait. The long rigors of migration were behind them.

This idyllic life of feeding, flying, and roosting is not all that it seems. The small body of water before me was packed with geese—more geese than would probably have roosted together in historic times. And each day the geese flew out to farm fields to feed on agricultural crops, whether or not the farmer liked it. While the hunting season was open they ran a gamut of guns, and many geese never saw the refuge again.

No chapter in the history of geese, especially of Canada geese, has needed rewriting in recent years so badly as the section that pertains to wintering behavior. By

While duck populations have decreased dramatically in recent decades due to nesting habitat loss, geese nest in northern areas unaffected by human activities and winter in protected habitats.

being evil or industrious, depending on your viewpoint, humankind has so refashioned the North American landscape that goose traditions thousands of years old have been altered nearly overnight. And the adaptable goose has made use of those changes, exhibiting an ability to respond more quickly than we could have imagined. They're lucky. Many species of birds have not fared so well. But that luck has come at the expense of free-ranging wildness, and has been paid for in the currency of controversy.

The human-induced changes that have affected behavior come in two forms—planned and accidental. Planned changes encompass such things as the establishment

of national wildlife refuges and similar state-owned reserves, and the re-establishment of extirpated populations. But these planned changes have triggered some unplanned results, such as overcrowding, disease, and short-stopping (geese refusing to fly as far south as they once did), demonstrating that even manipulated ecosystems are bound by the rule that all things are interdependent.

The accidental changes are largely the result of two human endeavors—agriculture and environmental destruction. To a smaller extent, environmental disruptions wrought by nature have also affected geese. Each change, whether purposeful or unintentional, has wrought even more changes.

OVERLEAF: Goose management has provided these geese with secure winter homes, but it has also altered ancient migration traditions.

This is not to infer that all is woe. Canada geese, as well as most other goose species, have never been so numerous. This story is truly one of the bright spots in wildlife management. But the lesson we're learning seems to be that the more we manage, the more management is needed; the life history of geese is now invariably tied to graphs, charts, meetings, surveys, and hunting regulations.

Refuges and Refugees

Though we have a tendency to think that environmental concern is something rather new, a consciousness that began with the first Earth Day on April 22, 1970, one of America's greatest conservation victories occurred in the 1930s, with the rapid expansion of the national wildlife refuge (NWR) system. Although immensely beneficial, and perhaps even critical, to the survival of migratory waterfowl, federal and state-owned refuges have forever changed the winter habits of geese—particularly Canada geese and, more recently, lesser snows.

Habitat loss has been at the root of the demise of most wildlife populations in recent times. For geese, habitat loss has occurred

A Rush For Refuges

The first national wildlife refuge was established in 1903. Located on the coast of Florida, Pelican Island was protected in order to save the nesting colony of birds for which it is named. But the next 30 years did not bode well for the refuge system—it languished for lack of funding. Not until the Dust Bowl era, not until drought and drainage ravaged the land, not until 1934 when President Franklin D. Roosevelt appointed a task force on wildlife restoration, was much more done.

But done it was. The task force, comprised of J.N. Darling, Aldo Leopold, and Thomas Beck, quickly pushed the concept of wildlife refuges and began to seek funding. Darling agreed to become the chief of the U.S. Biological Survey, forerunner to the Fish and Wildlife Service. Working feverishly, he scraped together $8.5 million, and a quarter of the sum came with the provision that it must be spent before the year was out. Darling also conceived and drew the first Migratory Bird Hunting Stamp, forever known as the Duck Stamp, which each waterfowl hunter had to purchase. Revenue from sale of the stamps was used to acquire wetlands.

Darling appointed J. Clark Salyer to survey wetlands for acquisition—a job Salyer completed in six weeks, driving alone over a distance of 18,000 miles and recommending 600,000 acres as refuge lands. The deadline was barely met, but when it was, waterfowl gained an important foothold for the future.

So critical are these refuges that it's doubtful we could have retained any semblance of historic waterfowl populations without them. Many refuges that were established after those first frantic acquisitions became necessary because of refinements in goose management, and because of the need to protect critical habitats.

There are 450 units of the national wildlife refuge system today, and more are under consideration. Important refuges for waterfowl also exist in Canada. Some refuges are well-known nationally, but others are treasures only to the wildlife they serve and to the people who live in the region.

Because they utilize farm crops, it's likely that geese have a more abundant food supply now than at any time in history.

primarily in migration and winter ranges. Because geese nesting in the far north have been spared, to date, the loss of breeding habitat that has driven duck populations to new lows, many goose populations probably exceed historical numbers.

The system of refuges across North America has provided protection for important migration habitat and wintering areas, though expanding goose populations are pushing the limits of these. With breeding habitat safe for the time being and hunting mortality regulated, it appears that southern migration and wintering habitat are the limiting factors in the growth of goose populations.

Geese learned quickly to use refuges,

due to a combination of factors. Hunting pressure on marshes that were not part of the system rapidly educated the geese to the benefits of roosting in a refuge. Destruction of marshes by farmers and developers made refuges attractive, and pollution and other forms of environmental degradation likewise limited options for geese. It's significant that geese were often first attracted to refuges with food provided by the managing agencies, crops at times manipulated to lure geese or to encourage them to move on. Regardless of the reason, along many migration routes and in a number of wintering areas, refuges are now the only game in town.

Refuges are not always pristine bits of

Wisconsin's Horicon Marsh, now a restored and important waterfowl migration habitat, was once destroyed when it was drained for farming purposes.

America. They may be reconstructions of historic marshes or new areas of habitat created to replace those lost. Some are on man-made impoundments, such as reservoirs. Sometimes refuges in the same flyway or migration corridor influence each other in dramatic ways. The histories of the Horicon Marsh and Horseshoe Lake refuges exemplify the intricacies of goose management.

The History of Horicon

Horicon Marsh, located 65 miles from Milwaukee in southeastern Wisconsin, totals nearly 32,000 acres. The northern part of the marsh is comprised of the 21,000-acre Horicon National Wildlife Refuge. To the

south, the state of Wisconsin manages the adjacent Horicon Marsh Wildlife Area, which covers an additional 11,000 acres.

To some of the Canada geese of the Hudson Bay nesting grounds, Horicon is an important place. Over 80 percent of the 1.1 million (1989 count) Mississippi Valley Population of Canada geese pause at Horicon during the autumn migration. Many also stop on their way north in March. Nearly 700,000 geese may be in or near Horicon during the peak of the fall flight. Horicon survives as one of the largest freshwater marshes in the United States, and it's certainly one of the largest cattail marshes in the world. On this wealth of water and marsh, and on the farm fields nearby, thousands of Canada geese converge. But it wasn't always this way.

Horicon evolved in a basin 14 miles long and up to five miles wide that the last glacier left in its wake. Impounded by a glacial moraine, meltwater flowed into the basin and created a lake. As time passed, erosion worked on the natural moraine dam, eventually permitting the waters to escape and leaving the progenitor marsh.

For 10,000 years, wildlife and man coexisted in and near the marsh. Then, in 1846, white settlers built a dam on the marsh outlet to power a sawmill, recreating the glacial lake and eradicating the marsh. The dam remained for 23 years until it was removed by judicial decree—the result of lawsuits filed by local farmers whose land had also been submerged.

When the waters returned to historic levels, waterfowl returned as well, leading to a dramatic increase in hunting pressure as private hunting clubs and market gunners converged on the marsh. By the time the 20th century rolled around, the wildlife of Horicon was nearly lost to unregulated, year-round gunning.

The wildlife was gone. Therefore, the marsh was without value in the eyes of many, and efforts turned to drainage. An elaborate system of ditches was dug over a four-year period; the main trench was over 14 miles long. Farmers moved in to till the marsh, only to find that their crops tasted like the peat soil, and that moisture in the spring and fall made planting and harvesting difficult.

The now-drained marsh was truly useless. Even the farmers abandoned it. When its peat soils caught fire, the marsh suffered its final indignation, as it smoldered for 12 years. Horicon was a foreboding place to both man and wildlife.

The Izaak Walton League of America, today one of the oldest conservation organizations but then in its infancy, began efforts to restore the marsh. Seven years of advocacy were rewarded in 1927, when the state legislature provided the funds needed to establish Horicon Marsh Wildlife Refuge. During an era when America was still ravaging its natural resources, the very notion of restoring a marsh (which had never before been attempted) seemed far-fetched, but it ultimately proved far-sighted.

A dam was built to flood the former marsh, and in 1934 the water returned to Horicon, quenching the burning peat. Nature responded rapidly, and dormant aquatic vegetation brought Horicon back to life. In 1941 the federal government acquired the remainder of Horicon. Today, 248 species of birds visit or live in the marsh.

Blues in the Bayou

"De goose, she doan come to de mawsh like dey used to," an old Cajun gentleman told me as he gazed across the vast coastal marsh behind his Louisiana bayou hunting camp. "When I was a leetle boy, dey was many Canada goose here. Now it is a beeg day when I see dem."

My Cajun friend's big days began to come less frequently with the changing pattern of Canada goose migration, largely because of that cyprus lake into which I had seen geese tumbling through trees. Historically, a great percentage of the Mississippi Valley Population's geese wintered in the deep south, spread across the huge Gulf Coast marshes. But Horseshoe Lake and other refuges changed all that.

In the 1920s Illinois waterfowl managers wondered if they could keep geese in the southern part of the state for a longer period of time by offering food and protection. In order to do this they established Horseshoe Lake Refuge, the heart of which is the lake that was once an oxbow bend of the Mississippi River. They acquired 3,500

OVERLEAF: Because there are now well-established refuges throughout the wintering range, the sight of flying geese is a common one during winter months in many parts of the U.S. and Canada.

acres of bottomland surrounding the lake, a dam was installed to keep the seasonally flooded lake permanently full, and managers began planting grain crops in the refuge to attract and feed the geese.

It was probably not long afterward that Cajun folks first noticed a decrease in goose numbers, for the plan to lure geese worked extremely well. Geese flocked to Horseshoe Lake. Held there by large quantities of food, the Canada geese paused for so long in the area that their instinct to migrate farther south simply faded.

As goose concentrations in the refuge area increased, so did hunting pressure until, in 1939, the kill was so large that authorities began to worry about its proportions. The hunting season was closed in 1945, as a result of unusually high mortality during the previous year's season— 5,000 geese were killed during the first five days.

Unsurprisingly, after the season was closed, goose numbers started to rebound. For the first time biologists realized that they could manipulate Canada goose populations by controlling the hunter harvest, and waterfowl management turned down a path that is followed yet today. Additionally, it was apparent that more refuges were needed in Illinois in order to spread out the huge concentration of geese at Horseshoe Lake, and within a few years Crab Orchard National Wildlife Refuge and the state-owned Union County Refuge came on-line to help ease the problem. Illinois was at the forefront of successful goose management, but that success was about to be short-circuited.

Just as the Illinois refuges short-stopped the geese from reaching the Gulf states, the new Horicon Marsh refuge farther north changed patterns to an even greater degree. Horicon was originally managed as a breeding grounds for the redhead duck. In the late 1940s, however, biologists began attracting Canada geese to the marsh, using the same techniques that had made Horseshoe Lake such a phenomenon. By the end of the decade, a few thousand geese stopped at Horicon. Two years later, as if the word had spread, over 100,000 geese paid a visit. Even when harsh weather swept in from the arctic, Canada geese were reluctant to leave Horicon. Folks further south in Illinois began to sing the sad Cajun's song when the geese didn't arrive until after the hunting season

The lack of geese in Illinois wasn't the only problem, though. Hunters followed the geese to Horicon, resulting in the same sort of large harvest experienced earlier at Horseshoe Lake. And geese weren't the only critters traveling in flocks, as tourists gathered along Highway 49 to watch the birds, creating traffic jams that stretched for miles. The huge flocks of geese tested the patience of farmers near Horicon by swarming into grain fields. Corporations and wealthy individuals began to tie up the surrounding lands in leases for private hunting clubs, limiting the availability of geese to the ordinary hunter. Because the geese were around in such numbers, the potential for serious overharvest loomed, and in fact such a harvest occurred in 1959, forcing a change in management practices.

Obviously, a migratory bird such as the Canada goose belongs to no one state or province. Aside from the possibility that Wisconsin hunters might be killing too many geese, it simply wasn't fair to keep these geese from bird watchers and hunters to the south. It was necessary to disperse the Mississippi Valley Population geese, both physically and harvest-wise, down the flyway.

Managers instituted zones around Horicon, in an attempt to more scientifically limit the number and location of goose kills during the hunting season, and they hoped hunting would encourage the geese to move south. But the birds were present in such

RIGHT: Given safe harbor and abundant food, wintering geese spend most of their time building vigor for the rigorous nesting season.

Canada geese have reached historically high numbers because of sound waterfowl management practices and their ability to feed on agricultural waste grain.

numbers that the total allowable kill for the entire fall often occurred during the first week; with hunting season then closed, the geese settled down to remain in the north. Extending the season would only lead to over-harvest, so managers were definitely in a quandary.

In 1966 an experimental program to drive the geese from Horicon began. Agency personnel set about hazing the geese, creating noise and disturbance in the hope that the geese would depart. The hazing only drove the geese to nearby areas, increasing hunting opportunities. Hunter success soared, the season once again closed early, and biologists learned another lesson about the intricacies of goose management.

Despite the fact that hunter success in the short-term was high, total goose kills were kept at a predetermined target level. But it was a period of adjustment for wildlife managers. During the decades of the '60s and '70s the goose population continued to grow. Refinements in refuge management were instituted. Elaborate hunting zones, each with specific season lengths and harvest quotas, became the norm up and down this flyway and others, and the seasons more accurately reflected the arrival of geese according to their new, refuge-influenced schedule. Habitat management at Horicon began to center more on wetlands than on food crops in order to lessen the effects of the geese being "on the dole," effects including nutritional deficiency, crop depredation, and altered migration patterns. But the instinct to home in on Horicon had become strong over the decades, and abundant foods were found in the surrounding farmlands, minimizing the success of efforts to force the geese to move. Today the geese remain in and near Horicon until weather drives them out, often until early December.

They do move eventually, driven on by the north wind. From refuge to refuge the geese go, but no more do large numbers winter in Cajun country. Initially attracted by refuge waters and the foods set out for them, Canada geese have found it difficult to push themselves away from the table, even after it becomes bare. Winter Canada geese are now largely welfare geese—refugees in their own refuges.

McCrops: Fast Food For Geese

Tied inexorably to the refuge system in encouraging the geese to spend winters farther north is the advent of agriculture in these regions, and the manner in which geese have adapted to feeding on farm crops. After all, Horicon Marsh existed historically, yet geese probably did not attempt to winter there, though it probably served as a migration stop. Prior to agriculture, inadequate food supplies meant that geese would not stay for the winter. Autumn and winter-dried grasses were insufficient to nurture a goose in cold weather, and the high-protein foods of the shallow marshes were locked in ice.

Today geese routinely feed on farm

Only when they're driven from northern refuges by a lack of food will most geese now venture into southern states.

As these tracks indicate, geese are well-suited for land-based grazing.

crops, which are high in energy and readily available until they're covered by snow. Dairy farm pastures near Horicon provide geese with high-quality forage. Illinois is also an agricultural state, so geese fly out to feed on winter wheat and corn. Atlantic Flyway Canada geese have also adapted their diet. Many feed on the farms of the Delmarva Peninsula (Delaware and Maryland) and fly to roost on Chesapeake and Delaware bays. If farmers try to switch crops to one that's less-favored by geese, the birds will simply modify their behavior.

For instance, Blackwater National Wildlife Refuge on Maryland's lower eastern shore was formerly the center for geese wintering in that state. When local farmers began to grow soybeans in the late 1970s, geese began to winter on the upper eastern shore where farmers grew corn, roosting on numerous farm ponds managed as sanctuaries.

The three populations of prairie Canada geese spend winter in the agriculturally intensive plains states, from Texas north through Missouri and even into South Dakota and Minnesota. Wherever they winter, the adaptable Canadas have swarmed to the upland fields for food.

As noted in earlier chapters, this trend has also been followed by other species of geese. White-fronted geese feed on rice extensively in both their California and

RIGHT: By hissing, this goose demonstrates its annoyance to an intruder.

Stretched out low in the water, a pair of Canada geese chooses to hide rather than confronting a threat.

Texas wintering grounds. Lesser snow geese mysteriously shifted to agricultural crops in California 30 years ago. The trend spread eastward throughout their population, and they now dine heavily on grains and the shoots of cereal crops wherever they winter.

The lesser snows have not only shifted diets; they've shifted wintering areas as well. Though the California population still winters in traditional locations (the largest of which is the Sacramento River Valley), midwestern snow geese now follow a pattern similar to Canada geese. Pausing frequently along the autumn migration route to feed on waste grains and shoots of winter wheat, they arrive in the south later than they did

in historical times. Nor do they fly as far south as they once did, though they don't winter quite as far north as Canada geese. Whereas the lessers once wintered mostly in the coastal marshes of Louisiana and Texas, the majority of mid-continent birds now spend winter in regions of those same states where rice is produced commercially, and farther north into Iowa, Missouri, Kansas, and Oklahoma.

Ross' geese have followed their cousins, the lesser snows, to the farm fields. Greater snow geese have been more reluctant to make the shift from their traditional diet of rushes to upland grazing, though it would not be surprising if they followed the trend of other geese. The Atlantic brant were forced to change their food habits when eelgrass mysteriously disappeared from their wintering range during the 1930s, but they've remained largely aquatic in their dining preference. Occasionally feeding on upland crops, Atlantic brant have today switched mostly to a diet of sea lettuce. Black brant of the Pacific have not faced the same shortage of eelgrass, but when infrequent scarcities occur they too switch to sea lettuce or upland meadow plants.

The massive dietary switch has both good and bad ramifications. Although geese mainly eat waste grain missed during harvest, many farmers claim that geese damage their crops—especially in the north, where geese may arrive before the harvest. When geese descend on a wheat crop that lays in swaths (piles of cut wheat like long windrows) they can devour much grain, although compaction and fouling the wheat with feces is probably a more serious problem, the result of geese standing atop the swaths while eating. However, with the advent of improved mechanical harvesters that allow crops to be cut and threshed in one operation, swathing has become a less common practice during harvest.

Another crop depredation complaint comes from farmers whose pastures attract geese. Because of their fondness for green forage, geese can damage sprouting crops which, under some circumstances, reduces the available forage for livestock, meaning that farmers must wait until the forage recovers before they can turn their animals loose on those acres.

In response to farmer complaints, financial compensation programs for crop losses have sprung up in areas with persistent problems. Though these programs only partially mitigate losses, farmers are generally satisfied. In Wisconsin farmers report a loss of $1.6 million annually, an average of over $1,000 per farm that claims damage. In parts of prairie Canada, lure crops or foods are used to draw geese and ducks away from farm fields until after the harvest.

Some biologists feel that these crop losses are exaggerated. In many regions agriculture and wildlife interests have been at war for decades over wetland issues. Sometimes the crop depredation issue has become a scapegoat for bad feelings, and the geese have been caught in the middle as highly visible symbols of the conflict between wildlife considerations and farm interests.

Other problems arise. Geese occasionally eat vegetation freshly treated with pesticides, paying a steep price for an easy meal. The insecticides diazinon and parathion have caused die-offs in geese. Anticholinesterase compounds applied to alfalfa have killed grazing geese through ingestion, inhalation, or dermal absorption of the toxin.

Geese are a social asset—a richness shared by us all. Geese flying overhead are a source of pleasure for everyone, including farmers. Geese can also become a source of income to landowners who charge fees to hunters wishing to use their land. And geese can actually increase the land's productivity by adding nutrients through defecation and by stimulating new plant growth through grazing.

Rice farmers in Arkansas who leave their paddies flooded (most drain the water from their fields in winter) are discovering that the multitudes of ducks and geese attracted to their fields consume noxious weeds and add free fertilizer, reducing the farmers' dependence on chemicals to do the same job. The practice of using fewer chemicals has in turn produced a marked improvement in water quality, benefiting both wildlife and the farm family.

A less-understood concern is what the switch in diet may do to a goose's health.

Though agricultural crops are important to today's goose, native moist-soil plants remain essential to balanced nutrition.

Man's crops are high-energy foods for geese. In some instances these crops can be considered "junk food." Native foods provide different nutrients than farm crops, such as calcium for egg shells, but they have been eradicated in much of the goose's wintering range.

Moist-soil plants such as knotweed and smartweed provide protein and essential amino acids, and studies seem to indicate that geese will feed frequently on such seeds when available. These nutrients become more important as the winter wanes and the geese need to get in top physical condition for the flight north and nesting. Many populations of geese add these foods and the green shoots of grasses (wild and domestic) to their diets as spring nears, in order to achieve proper nutrition. However, corn and other grains are still consumed for fast weight gain.

The problem is that the type of wetland habitats in which the native foods grow are also those most often targeted for destruction. Shallow, gradually sloping, and only seasonally flooded, these wetlands are easy to drain and are easily converted to croplands. Losses have been staggering, amounting to millions of acres across North America. Managers are currently working to provide more of this type of habitat, both along migration routes and near wintering areas. Such an approach spreads out goose populations, gives them a more diverse and healthy diet, and adds habitats that are beneficial to a wide range of wildlife.

The creation of new refuges and the restoration of marsh habitats eases goose management problems in a number of ways. Crop depredation is not perceived by farmers as such a serious problem when it happens irregularly, or when it's caused by smaller numbers of geese. Diet is diversified when geese can feed on native foods in restored habitats. Hunting pressure is spread out, and the quality of the hunt is improved. Finally, the more habitat there is, the less crowded geese will be, minimizing the chance of catastrophic contagion and other calamities.

Disease and Disasters

Contagious diseases can locally affect large numbers of waterfowl. As habitat decreases and ducks and geese are crowded together, the likelihood of an outbreak increases. Habitat loss does not cause disease, any more than a day care center for children causes colds. But the increase in proximity in both cases leads to rapid transmission of illness once an infected individual enters the crowd. Two particularly dangerous and relatively common waterfowl diseases are avian cholera and avian botulism.

Avian cholera is transmitted through the water from bird to bird, and is believed to stem from direct or indirect contact (such as farm run-off entering a wetland frequented by wildfowl) with the domestic fowl that carry this disease. Once an infected goose or duck returns to the water to roost, cholera can spread rapidly through crowded habitats. Sick waterfowl have difficulty breathing, as mucus builds up in the respiratory tract. Death comes relatively quickly.

Although most commonly associated with the western half of the United States, avian cholera has occurred across the continent, with outbreaks as widespread as Maine, Minnesota, Texas, Nebraska, and California. Some outbreaks can hit geese populations hard. A spring flare-up in 1980 killed nearly 80,000 white-fronted, lesser snow, and Canada geese that had paused in Nebraska on their way north. The disease remains an annual problem in the area. Avian cholera has recently plagued Lac qui Parle Refuge in Minnesota. An estimated 7,200 Canada geese succumbed to the disease on this lake in 1989, and 6,600 died in 1991.

Avian botulism also takes its toll. This toxic bacteria is activated in dry, warm conditions when water levels are low. As oxygen is depleted in the warm waters, spores germinate and feed on dead animal matter. As ducks and geese die, they provide even more nursery areas in which the toxic maggots can grow. Large numbers of waterfowl succumb to the disease, and only the onset of cool, wet weather can avert disaster.

One of the largest outbreaks of avian botulism occurred in California's Central Valley, where an estimated 250,000 birds died during the winter of 1968-69. Manitoba's Whitewater Lake, an important autumn migration area for geese, was the scene of outbreaks that claimed 50,000 waterfowl during the early 1960s.

When infected by botulism, waterfowl suffer a slow paralysis that affects their internal organs and legs first, followed by loss of strength in the neck. Ironically, these wonderful water birds eventually drown because they can no longer keep their heads above water. Aside from praying for cold weather and rain, waterfowl managers can do little more than gather up the dead and dying birds, burning or burying the carcasses to slow the spread of botulism.

Nebraska's Rainwater Basins: Critical Habitat

A perfect example of how important a single type of habitat can be, and of the effects of crowding wildlife onto it, can be seen in the Rainwater Basins of Nebraska.

Before agriculture prevailed, perhaps as many as a quarter-million acres of these shallow, wind-formed depressions existed in the south-central part of the state. Nearly all but the largest, hardest-to-drain wetlands were converted to agriculture, until a scant 34,000 acres remain today.

Despite the fact that the acreage has dwindled, and that in many cases the quality of the wetlands has suffered, the Rainwater Basins serve an amazing array of waterfowl from the three westernmost flyways each year, particularly as spring staging habitat.

Geese move north each spring to these early-opening wetlands, beginning in late February. Depending on the weather, geese will remain and feed intensively for up to three weeks, scavenging waste corn from nearby farms and consuming great quantities of wetland plants such as smartweed. These plants are high in protein and other nutrients, and the geese eat not only eat the seeds of smartweed—they uproot and consume the entire plant. During their stay in the Basins, geese may add up to a pound of body fat; that's 20 percent of a typical snow goose's entire weight. The extra weight and added nutrients are critical to nesting success.

Canada, white-fronted, and lesser snow geese all make extensive use of these wetlands. At the peak of the spring migration during the second week in March, two million geese inhabit the region simultaneously, spread across those few thousand remaining wetland acres. According to estimates, 90 percent of the mid-continental population of white-fronted geese may gather together on the Basins at the same time. Snow geese from both the Central and Mississippi flyways use the Basins—nearly one million at their peak. Half a million Canadas make the same stop, and an unknown number of Ross' geese pause here. In addition, hundreds of thousands of ducks and sandhill cranes occupy the same wetlands.

Such crowding has led to disasters. Outbreaks of avian cholera have become an annual event over the last couple of decades. In a good year, biologists are happy to see the death toll contained to 2,000 geese. Losses of 5,000 to 8,000 waterfowl annually are not uncommon, and the vast majority of the casualties are geese. The worst case on record happened in 1980, when nearly 80,000 died.

With geese gathered in such dense congregations, conditions are ripe for disaster. For 2-1/2 hours on the evening of March 13, 1990, a severe tornado cut a path of death through the Rainwater Basins. Waterfowl concentrations were at their peak, and when the roaring storm reached them, the geese rose in panic. The storm caught them in the air, and as many as 30,000 geese died. In the town of York, dead geese actually rained down from the sky. State workers filled the bed of a pickup truck with carcasses of geese found along just a one-mile stretch of highway. The majority of geese killed were snow geese, but white-fronted geese died in high proportion to their total numbers.

Efforts are underway in Nebraska to double the number of Basin acres through restoration and enhancement. As part of the North American Waterfowl Management Plan, work will be done on newly acquired wetlands and on private lands, providing marshes and uplands to better nurture the geese and ducks, and to minimize the sometimes disastrous effects of crowding.

RIGHT: The sight of thousands of geese flocked together is exciting, but loss of habitat has sometimes forced geese to become crowded. The risk of disaster and disease is increased in such conditions.

Concentrations of wildlife can also be subject to unexpected disasters that quickly kill thousands. For instance, an unusual onslaught of cold weather caught the Atlantic brant by surprise during the period between 1976 and 1978, and the birds did not adapt readily. Nearly 90,000 brant starved to death, unable to feed because of ice conditions.

Though disasters and disease can certainly take their toll on geese, by far the largest cause of mortality is a conscious act committed by people—hunting.

The Goose as Game Bird

The passion I personally feel for hunting is not mine alone. It's a passion shared by millions, though it has come under scrutiny in recent years. Some non-hunting people vehemently oppose the sport; others have few qualms about hunting if it's done responsibly.

Wildlife managers use hunting as an integral part of goose management. Indeed, the greatest effort of those responsible for managing North America's goose populations is directed toward censusing the birds, then deriving and enforcing hunting regulations based on those census numbers.

The goal is two-fold. First, goose populations need to be maintained for their own benefit, so that geese can achieve their full reproductive potential. Second, regulations attempt to provide an equitable harvest of geese throughout their migratory and winter ranges. Both of these targets are further influenced by the need to protect races or species that are in trouble and, conversely, to control goose populations that are too large, threatening their own wintering or breeding grounds or becoming a local nuisance.

Scientists working with the various goose species and in the four flyways routinely create "population objectives," which are nothing more than target numbers for partic-

ular populations of geese, numbers based on the carrying capacity of available habitats in both the wintering and breeding areas. Population objectives change from time to time in order to accommodate changes in habitat and the results of serious weather problems faced by nesting geese. In other words, a poor hatch in a snowbound nesting ground will influence the length and bag limit of the hunting season to follow, so that the geese are protected. Loss of habitat would create a similar scenario.

While this formula sounds straightforward, the task of determining population numbers is not a simple one. Surveys are done annually to judge the health of the goose populations and to assess conditions on the breeding grounds. Depending on the species of goose, the survey can take place either in winter or spring, whenever and wherever species gather in large groups. Usually this is done from the air by experienced counters flying over known gathering areas. In order to avoid the possibility that birds moving from one refuge to another may be counted twice, the census is done over a short period of time and is taken by as many as 1,000 wildlife professionals working simultaneously.

Because so many variables come into play, the winter survey can't offer a total count of goose populations—it's more of a general indicator. The survey also assesses the conditions of winter habitat. When waterfowl suddenly quit using one area, such a switch may be an important ecological indicator of the land's health—an aspect important not only to geese, but ultimately to us.

Breeding ground surveys are conducted in much the same manner, but because the birds aren't nearly so concentrated, the process takes a much longer time. While the breeding ground surveys are critical in estimating duck populations (ducks are more

LEFT: During winter, the goose's family unit remains intact.

difficult to census in the winter because they don't congregate like geese), their primary relevance to geese lies in determining the potential for nesting success. Since this potential is controlled primarily by weather and flooding, aerial surveys examine the breeding grounds for late snow cover or for excessive amounts of run-off that could delay nesting or destroy nests.

Once the winter population is known and the nesting conditions have been determined, biologists can add the known reproductive potential of the species, ending up with a fairly accurate picture of the fall flight. The population objective is the number at which managers would like to see the fall flight maintained. Nature operates in cycles: Populations climb until a creature becomes too numerous, at which time disease or starvation drastically reduces numbers. Because people deem an abundant goose population to be a good thing, population objectives seek to keep the goose numbers stable—high enough to meet the public demand, but below the threshold at which habitat would be destroyed or disease would run rampant.

After the population objective has been ascertained, managers can prescribe a reasonable harvest of surplus geese. The portion of the goose population labeled "surplus" refers to the number of birds in excess of the amount of breeding geese required to maintain a healthy population. Season lengths and bag limits are set in a manner that will allow the harvest of surplus birds without damaging the total population. Limits and season vary dramatically throughout North America, reflecting regional goose management and special species concerns.

When goose populations are at high levels, hunting mortality is viewed as "compensatory," meaning that birds killed by hunters would in any case have died during the year from other causes. Thus, mortality remains relatively constant, though the means differ. If a goose population is suffering decline from other causes and drops to a low number, hunting mortality becomes additive and can contribute to the decline. In these instances, seasons are closed or shortened, bag limits are reduced, or some combination of the above occurs.

Obviously, management is complicated, and fine lines must be walked. The fact that goose populations have continued to spiral upward despite some annual fluctuations indicates that hunting has not had an adverse effect on population in recent decades. If our management success is to continue, though, we must rely on intensive studies and complicated regulations. These haven't always been in place.

Poorly regulated or unregulated hunting has hurt goose populations in the past, even driving the giant Canada goose to near-extinction levels. Much of the damage was done by market gunners who killed geese for sale to restaurants and grocers. Greater snow and Ross' geese were reduced to only a few thousand each by the early 1900s. And as late as 1971, Atlantic brant suffered serious declines due to a high harvest coupled with nearly complete failure on the breeding grounds.

The Mississippi Valley Population of Canada geese was reduced to a winter total of less than 30,000 in 1946, largely because of excessive hunting. Today, the same population contains about a million Canada geese and continues to grow, thanks to better wintering ground management and hunting regulations. Similar scenarios have occurred in the three other flyways and for most species of geese.

Perhaps the greatest challenge to wildlife managers in charge of hunting seasons is how to protect troubled subspecies of geese that winter with lookalike cousins. To a hunter huddled in a blind, one Canada goose looks much like the next. Therefore,

RIGHT: Paradoxically, today's abundance of geese is due in large part to the purchase of Duck Stamps and hunting licenses. Revenues are used to acquire refuges and to fund research, management, and wetland preservation projects.

OVERLEAF: The sight of geese flying en masse against the backdrop of a prairie sunset is an inspiring one.

protecting the rare dusky Canada while allowing the harvest of other, more numerous races with which it winters in regions of western Oregon and southwestern Washington is a complex matter. Elaborate banding studies have now defined those places where the dusky Canada congregates, leading to the creation of zones that protect the dusky while allowing hunting in other zones.

Another problem involves non-migrating populations of Canada geese, which are generally more susceptible to hunting pressure than migratory populations. Because of their attachment to certain habitats, they're less likely to abandon them even in the face of hunting. Migrating populations with no particular attachment to these spots simply choose areas where hunting pressure is low or nonexistent.

In some cases the resident flocks need harvesting because they have become nuisances. At other times, in spots where flocks are just being established, they require protection. Managers must first define which races and species use which habitats, then try to weave a web of regulations and zones that allow for hunting, are understandable, and protect those geese that need protection.

Goose hunting is a means by which wildlife managers can exercise control of goose numbers, gather information, and gain critical funding. The hunter's return of leg and neck bands from bagged geese is fundamental to the success of studies that seek to determine the dynamics of population, age, and sex, and that locate the breeding and wintering grounds of geese.

A federal excise tax on hunting equipment is returned to agencies that fund research programs, and the sale of over two million Federal Duck Stamps each year (a required purchase for all duck and goose hunters over the age of 16), serves as the primary source of dollars for the national wildlife refuges. Since its inception in 1934, nearly four million acres of wetlands have been acquired through the Duck Stamp program. Many states have adopted a similar program within the last two decades, and state duck stamps purchased by hunters have been critical to the development of state waterfowl programs and wetland preservation efforts. Canada has instituted a similar nationwide stamp system.

Waterfowl hunters comprise a large, vocal group that advocates wetland protection. Hunters that belong to organizations such as Ducks Unlimited, the Izaak Walton League, and Goose International are an important voice for waterfowl and their habitats. Nationally, hunters spend millions of dollars per year in rural areas while on hunting trips, proving to local agricultural interests that a tangible, financial benefit can be gained by making room for wildlife on their lands.

But no matter how one feels about hunting, there is an act that everyone should abhor—poaching. Annually, poachers acting illegally kill many geese simply for financial profit.

Funds For Friends

Each year the United States spends approximately $2.4 billion on wildlife conservation. As impressive as that total sounds, it's rarely enough to fund all the worthwhile conservation programs.

Three-fourths of America's wildlife budget is contributed directly or indirectly by the nation's hunters, anglers, and trappers. Most of this $1.8 billion is derived from license fees and from the federal excise tax on equipment these people purchase; the balance comes in the form of donations from conservation groups—some $300 million annually. Ducks Unlimited alone spends about $68 million per year.

RIGHT: Though a goose's life may be simple, its relationship to humankind is much studied and managed.

Goose Slaughter

Geese belong to no one. They don't belong to the wealthy or irresponsible as objects of slaughter. They deserve, at the very least, fair play and an opportunity to outsmart people, as they generally do in a hunting situation. Poached geese are baited; lured to their death in ponds or fields baited with grain. Baiting is always illegal. Swatting—shooting at a flock of sitting geese—is reprehensible. Poaching operations run the gamut from a backwoods opportunist who makes a few extra bucks to large-scale operations run by organized crime, which is increasingly involved in wildlife poaching. In any event, responsible waterfowl management becomes impossible in the face of significant poaching.

The problem is complex. Some district attorneys feel wildlife protection laws are unimportant, and therefore don't prosecute violations. Federal magistrates may hand down inadequate sentences, thereby sending the message that poaching isn't regarded as a serious crime. Judges are sometimes openly hostile toward wildlife special agents who dare to bring cases to court. According to one agent who asked to remain anonymous, "There are some courts where, when we go to trial, I don't know who's going to end up in jail—me or the defendant."

The Division of Law Enforcement for the U.S. Fish and Wildlife Service has been getting little support from its own parent agency, from non-government conservation organizations, or from the general public. For instance, while the staff of the USFWS has increased by 78 percent since 1977, the total number of law enforcement special agents has dropped by eight percent. And while the budget for 1992 gave the USFWS a 21 percent increase, no increase was given to law enforcement. The agency's Division of Law Enforcement has dwindled to just 180 agents in the field; these overburdened individuals are in charge of protecting our wildlife and enforcing all aspects of endangered plant and species laws.

Geese become a target for poachers primarily in their wintering areas. If the poacher is to kill large numbers of birds, the birds have to be present in large numbers. During migration, illegal kills of geese are small—usually committed by unscrupulous hunters who are not satisfied with the legal limit. Only in wintering grounds across the country can large-scale slaughters occur, and then only in places where the public turns its back.

The ultimate casualties are, of course, the geese themselves. Those of us who love and admire geese, whether we hunt or simply enjoy the sound of their passing symphony, need to make sure that these birds receive the protection they deserve. If society decides that poaching is unacceptable and insists that tough, fair sentences must be imposed by the judicial system, the practice will end. Until that day, the unscrupulous will continue to slaughter not just geese, but other remarkable wildlife as well.

● ● ●

Down the flyways through the winter, the story of the wild goose has become as complex as our own harried lives. Though the geese seek to do only what they have always done—prepare themselves to raise yet another generation—they increasingly contend with human endeavors and plans.

From the goose's perspective, life remains pretty simple. To the majority of people, necks bent back, eyes wide open in a wondering gaze, geese are pure magic and wildness. But no longer will the geese fly south subject only to a wondering gaze. In a world in which the natural order has forever been changed, geese will have to be managed—for their own good and to help them avoid conflicts with humans.

Whether they benefit from our management is a matter for each of us to oversee, and to judge.

LEFT: Our wealth of geese is a resource that deserves respect, and it should be protected from unscrupulous exploitation.

CHAPTER FIVE

THE ONCE AND FUTURE GOOSE

Geese Too Few

There was a time, not so many decades ago, when the sight of geese was a much rarer occurrence. Market gunning, poor hunting management, and habitat loss had driven goose populations to historic lows. Though we often view the past with wistfulness, those who love geese need not. We are now living in "the good old days" with respect to geese. With three million Canada geese on the continent, over two million lesser snow geese, and up to 400,000 white-fronted geese, goose lovers today, wherever they may live, rarely lack for an opportunity to watch these spectacular birds. And the prospects are generally rosy for the future.

Populations are likely to increase as intensive efforts maintain the quality of wintering habitat, as the birds themselves adapt to winter foods found in farmer's fields, and as most breeding grounds continue to evade development because they're so remote. The goose today is a symbol of sound wildlife management combined with ardent public support. Geese are also the picture of adaptability and the epitome of luck.

Despite all the good news, there are some geese whose status is threatened. Interestingly, these geese nest in Alaska—a wild state that few of us would imagine has been altered enough to cause problems for wildlife. Not surprisingly, these races of Canada geese are in trouble mostly due to habitat changes caused by both humans and natural events.

The endangered Aleutian Canada goose (*B.c. leucopareia*) once nested on many small islands in the Aleutian chain, from Kodiak Island west across the entire Aleutian and Commander island arc. Some were even found as far south as the central Krile Islands of Asia, which made them the only naturally occurring population of Canada geese found outside of the North American continent.

This small-bodied race of Canada goose suffered tremendous losses when arctic and red foxes were introduced into their habitat from 1910 to 1930 by islanders who wanted to raise foxes for furs. Unable to withstand predation from the opportunistic fox, Aleutian geese were nearly eliminated from their former nesting sites and were thought to be extinct as early as 1930. Not until 1962, when biologists found a remnant band of 300 breeding geese on fox-free Buldir Island, was there proof that this race had not suffered the same fate as the passenger pigeon.

Discovering the remnant geese, though exciting, was only the first step in ensuring that extinction did not occur. The U.S. Fish and Wildlife Service moved in and live-trapped some of the geese, which were then transported to the agency's facility in Patuxent, Maryland. These captive, protected geese were kept for breeding, and their offspring were to be later reintroduced to their ancestral range. In the meantime, foxes were removed from the Aleutian goose's breeding islands through an active trapping program. Biologists simultaneously studied the breeding behavior of the remaining wild stock, and banding studies were initiated to determine the Aleutian's migration routes and wintering areas—information necessary in order to devise ways that the geese could be protected from hunters who were legally pursuing abundant, lookalike Canada geese races.

The banding studies revealed that the Aleutian goose migrated mostly to the northern coast of California, in the vicinity

LEFT: The giant Canada goose was first thought to be only a myth; it was then believed to be extinct. Its current proliferation serves as an abundant testimony to the success of wildlife management.

of Crescent City, and to the Sacramento Valley near Colusa before eventually moving to their winter residence near Modesto in the San Joaquin Valley. Another small group wintered on the northern Oregon coast near Netarts Bay. Once the migration and winter habitat had been defined, regulations were implemented forbidding all Canada goose hunting during the period when the Aleutians were present in these regions. In California these restrictions began in 1975; similar rules were in place in Oregon by 1982.

Slowly, the research, the fox trapping, the studies, and the protection began to pay off. By 1975 the population had inched upward to about 750 individuals. In 1983 and 1984, two additional surviving breeding colonies were found in the Semidi Islands and the eastern Aleutian island of Chagulak. New colonies were established on three other islands by using relocated stock of trapped wild geese, and through releases of offspring from the captive birds reared in Maryland. By 1991 there were over 6,000 Aleutian Canada geese.

Aleutian geese continue to expand their range, which puts them in a much less precarious position than they were in just a couple of decades ago. The day is nearing when their official status can be downgraded from endangered to threatened. The majority of the population increase has taken place on islands west of the range of the bald eagle—the most deadly predator of Aleutian geese other than foxes. Eagles have always fed on geese, of course, but goose numbers are low enough that attempts to establish nests on islands inhabited by eagles usually end in disaster for the geese. At one time, the sheer number of geese rendered eagle predation relatively insignificant, but when only a few geese are present, eagles make it difficult for the geese to venture into new areas.

But the future isn't completely secure. Although several state and federal reserves have been acquired in the wintering range in order to provide habitat for these rare geese, more habitat is needed, and wildlife interests have to compete with wealthier factions seeking to acquire land for other purposes. Even near the already-secured habitat in development-crazed California, farmlands in which the geese feed are rapidly being turned into home and business sites. And wetland loss in the state is staggering. During the period from 1780 to 1980, 91 percent of California's wetland acres were destroyed, drastically reducing the winter habitat for waterfowl in the Pacific Flyway. The U.S. Fish and Wildlife Service estimates that, historically, California contained five million wetland acres (five percent of the state's total acreage). Today, less than 500,000 acres remain.

A Dusky Disaster

Meanwhile, on the southern coast of Alaska, another race of Canada goose faces serious problems. The green and grey maze of marsh at the mouth of the Copper River, backed by black mountains and starkly striped by bands of snow, is the major nesting ground of the dusky Canada goose (*B.c. occidentalis*). Untouched by humans, the nesting grounds are nonetheless in serious trouble as the result of a natural cataclysm.

The Good Friday earthquake of 1964 not only sent shock waves through human communities in Alaska, but dealt a blow to the Copper River Delta, lifting this area upward by as much as ten feet. A change in vegetation occurred as marsh became high ground. A continuing succession of plants covered the former marsh, dramatically changing its characteristics and inviting new animals to make use of the delta. The dusky geese, however, still homed in on this ancestral breeding ground.

RIGHT: The Alaskan nesting ground of this dusky Canada goose is in serious trouble due to a natural cataclysm.

Wetlands Down the Drain

Wetlands have only recently become a "sexy" political and environmental issue, although conservation groups such as Ducks Unlimited and the Izaak Walton League of America have been fighting to preserve these areas for decades. America rarely responds to an issue until it's faced with a crisis. That a wetlands crisis exists is a notion that some pro-development and agricultural interests still dispute. But the evidence against them is staggering.

When settlers first landed on the eastern seaboard, the area that now constitutes the lower 48 states contained an estimated 221 million acres of wetlands. These swamps, potholes, marshes, and bogs were viewed as wastelands to be filled, drained, or used as dumps. For the next 200 years, America waged war on wetlands.

By the 1980s, the lower 48 states had lost about 53 percent of their original wetlands. Figured another way, during the 200-year period from 1780 to 1980, one acre was lost per minute!

For waterfowl, the losses were critical. Some of the greatest destruction came in areas where geese and ducks spend the winter—in California, Arkansas, and Louisiana. Small wetlands critical for breeding ducks and as a source of pre-nesting nutrients for northbound geese were those easiest to destroy, and therefore were most commonly lost. Since these wetlands are flooded only seasonally, pro-drainage forces commonly assert that they should not qualify as wetlands and should not be protected. However, temporary wetlands are among the most fertile.

One-third of all wetland destruction—over 36 million acres—occurred in the midwestern farm belt. The vast majority of this wetland loss was funded by the average citizen through federal programs that encouraged farmers to drain these areas and convert them to croplands. Besides spending our tax dollars in the form of cash incentives, government agencies provided technical support for the farmer. Cash subsidies for crops further encouraged conversion of more wetlands into farm fields. And despite all the talk in recent years, we continue to lose wetlands at an unacceptable rate.

Wetlands are valuable to people, even if the wildlife factor is not considered. Wetlands help maintain groundwater levels and purity; they protect shorelines from erosion; they store flood waters and trap sediments; and they help moderate climatic change.

Because ducks and geese are so closely monitored and counted, they serve as indicator species for wetland health and abundance. Whatever fate befalls waterfowl will certainly befall hundreds of other creatures that also depend upon wetlands for survival. Human destiny, too, is inextricably tied to the fate of wildlife. And so, ultimately, what's good for the goose is good for us.

Wetland preservation efforts are critical to the future of waterfowl. They also benefit people in many ways.

LEFT: The wetland complexes that this goose and millions of other waterfowl depend upon have rapidly been disappearing.

Some of the new animals frequenting the delta found the geese and their eggs delectable, and the dusky was soon in trouble as wolves and brown bears sidled up to the dinner table. For years the dusky population spiraled downward. With winter mortality due to hunting and, in some years, nearly no recruitment of young to the population, the picture became grim.

Enter the U.S. Forest Service and Ducks Unlimited. The Forest Service is the agency in charge of the Copper River Delta area, which is located in the Chugach National Forest. Researchers began to install various types of artificial nesting structures, most of them in the form of "islands." Some are simply sandbags, while others are floating platforms. Geese nesting on these safe bits of habitat enjoyed a much better success rate than those nesting on the altered uplands, because the surrounding waters acted as a barrier to most predators. In some years, the difference is astounding: In 1989, for example, geese enjoyed 57 percent nesting success on islands, compared to just four percent success on shore.

Ducks Unlimited and the Forest Service have teamed up to install over 800 nesting structures based on this success, but production has been sporadic to date. Mid-winter population counts from 1984 through 1990 estimated the total dusky number at between 7,500 and 12,000. Almost all of these geese winter in the Willamette Valley and lower Columbia River region of Washington and Oregon. In addition to the change in habitat on the breeding grounds, dusky geese still face decline due to hunting mortality. The latter is in large part due to the complicated nature of the goose's changing wintering habits.

For instance, in the decades of the '50s and '60s, the winter flock in this region of Washington and Oregon was made up almost entirely of dusky geese. Protecting geese in such a scenario is simple: Close the hunting season in that particular locale. But by the '70s, large numbers of the numerous Taverner's Canada geese (*B.c. taverneri*), which nest across interior Alaska, began to use the same wintering grounds. By 1984 they comprised 85 percent of the flock. In addition, western (*B.c. moffitti*) and cackling (*B.c. minima*) Canada geese began to mix in. The cackling goose itself was driven to near-threatened status as recently as 1983, because of harvest by hunters in the south combined with harvest by the Yupik eskimos on its nesting grounds.

With the increased number of geese wintering in Washington and Oregon, crop depredation problems multiplied. No longer was closing the hunting season an option—area farmers saw the hunting season as a way to control the goose population and minimize crop losses. Yet, though the Taverner's goose was plentiful, both the dusky and the cackling goose needed protection. Experimental seasons designed to protect these geese while permitting harvest of other, more numerous geese yielded mixed results. Too many adult duskys were harvested, as far as many biologists were concerned.

Refinements in hunting zones and regulations are continuing, in an effort to lower mortality among dusky and cackling geese. Despite the success of the artificial nesting islands, the dusky Canada goose remains troubled, as the number of young hatched each year serves to slow the decline but does not reverse the trend.

The problems facing these races of Canada geese are complex. Altered habitats may never return to the productivity of pristine environments. Land use conflicts in the south, combined with rampant development and continued loss of wetlands, result in crowded geese and conflicts with human interests. These southern conflicts will only grow as the human population

RIGHT: Managing Canada geese is not a simple task. One complicating factor is the need to protect troubled races such as this cackling goose while allowing for the harvest of abundant look-alike races in order to reduce crop depredation.

grows. Over-harvest remains a danger because, on the wing, the threatened geese are virtually identical to other races of Canada geese, and some inevitably end up in the hunter's bag.

The Aleutian and dusky Canada geese have dribbled around the abyss of extinction, but there is one Canada goose that actually became "extinct." Now, however, there are too many of these geese. How is that possible? Read on.

The Mythological Goose

Ten thousand years ago, the last glaciers retreated north after they had swept south to what is now the northern plains. In their wake they left footprints—uncounted millions of acres of marshlands, large and small, dotting what would become prairie.

Life rapidly adapted to this new habitat. Birds made use of the prairie potholes, ecosystems so fertile that 130 different species might use a single wetland in the span of a year. Waterfowl, particularly ducks, found these wetlands the ultimate breeding grounds. Too numerous to count, the potholes allowed each of the more territorial species to claim a secure and separate nesting site in nearby grassy uplands. The diverse potholes, ranging from shallow spring sheet water to permanent prairie lakes, provided perfect habitats for each stage of nesting and brood development. Located mostly in what is now the north-central United States and extreme south-central Canada, the prairie pothole region offered long, warm summers, leaving waterfowl ample time to raise a brood. Fifty percent of the continent's ducks were produced in these prairie wonders, and one race of goose regarded them as home as well.

Throughout the potholes and lakes of this region, and eventually into the river watersheds, the Canada goose nested. But not just any Canada goose. Supported by a lush habitat and enjoying a long growing season, this Canada goose evolved into the biggest of its kind, averaging about 12 pounds and with individuals approaching twenty. Like everything else in this massive landscape, this goose was big. It was a giant, the giant—the giant Canada goose (*B.c. maxima*).

Waterfowl weren't the only numerous creatures on the prairies. Vast herds of bison, elk, and antelope ran free on the grasslands region, which rivaled in size and grandeur any grassland on the planet, the equal of Africa's Serengeti Plain. Sixty million or more bison moved in thundering herds, creating great, groaning waves of migrating mammals. Though they didn't know it, the bison were working in concert with the geese that watched them from the wetlands. Indeed, they were the goose's benefactor.

The milling herds of bison grazed the tall prairie grasses. What they didn't eat, they trampled. But they practiced a natural, deferred-grazing rotation, moving on to new areas and not returning to a spot until new grasses had grown. What they left in their wake were foods to which other creatures adapted. Antelope loved the flowering plants that bison rejected; also following in the bison's wake, after rain and sun had started the new, green grass shooting toward the sky, was the grazing goose—the giant Canada—feeding on the tender greenery.

This relationship could probably have lasted forever, with the black and white geese always following the dusty brown herds of bison to new pastures, except for one factor—the European settler.

Europeans did not view bison as the source of life, as did the Plains Indians. Instead, the new settlers envisioned replacing bison with cattle, and sought to substitute amber waves of grain for flowing grasslands. Europeans were quite aware as well that, in order to remove the Indian people, removal

LEFT: Though the populations of some Canada goose races are low, when all races are considered it's likely that there are more Canada geese on this continent than at any point in history.

OVERLEAF: When European settlers first came west, they discovered a seemingly endless supply of geese.

The giant Canada goose shared the prairies with millions of bison, eating the new grass shoots that sprung up on bison-grazed land. When the bison were slaughtered, the geese suffered from lack of food.

of their principal food source—the bison—was necessary.

What followed was an environmental holocaust that rivals anything that happened before or has happened since. The same nation that today bemoans the conversion of African plains to cows and crops, that laments the slaughter of elephants, eradicated the bison in *just a decade*. The large majority of the 60 million bison died, in fact, in a three-year frenzy of destruction, shot and then sold for their skins by an army of market gunners.

The bison just barely escaped extinction before the massacre ended, but the Indian way of life didn't fare so well. Nor did

the giant Canada goose. Without enough grazing partners to ensure a source of fresh greenery, populations of giants declined. If they had been able to sustain themselves until grain fields and pasture lands replaced the tall, ungrazed grasses, they might have rebounded. But they weren't to be so lucky.

Settlers followed the buffalo gunners to these prairies. When they did, they saw geese as either a subsistence food source or as a way to make money through sale of meat. It's possible, though, to understand why in those days the possibility of a bird's extinction never crossed people's minds. After all, each autumn, millions of seemingly identical geese migrated through this region. The supply of geese appeared to be endless.

But the giant Canada geese were a discreet population, spread out in small groups over a wide area and completely separate from their northern relatives. Like all geese, they had a strong homing tendency. When a settler shot a pair of geese on a nearby pothole to feed his family, he eliminated all breeders from that marsh. A million geese overhead meant nothing to that empty wetland, for those geese were bound for their own breeding grounds in the arctic. No new giants would move in to replace the lost pair; there were none to spare, for across their range giant Canadas were suffering the same fate. Because the entire population had already declined from the loss of bison grazing partners, there were no surplus geese to pioneer into empty habitats.

The wild breeding pairs eventually disappeared. With them went the giant Canada goose, *Branta canadensis maxima*, vanishing before it could even be given the name. Or so everyone thought.

Persistent reports trickled in each year, funneled to the eyes and ears of biologists and ornithologists, of large Canada geese occasionally bagged by hunters. Birds weighing 12, 15, 18, and even 20 pounds were reported. Most reports were regarded as rumors, attributed to inaccurate scales, or dismissed as the outright lies of bragging waterfowlers. Decades passed. The rumored species was listed as extinct in 1947, and some wondered if it had ever existed. Even then, though, some doubted its demise.

In the meantime, wildlife management was becoming a science. Across America, biologists were poking and prodding into all corners, studying everything, cataloging and weighing specimens. Some of these explorers were about to make an important discovery.

In the southeastern Minnesota city of Rochester, famed for its Mayo Clinic, a dam had been built on the Zumbro River. The resulting body of water, Silver Lake, became home for a band of geese, some of which were progeny of a semi-domesticated flock of Canada geese raised by Dr. Charles H. Mayo, Sr., as a hobby. The city bought a few of the domesticated geese to put in its 25-acre lake.

A patient at the Mayo Clinic, who had enjoyed seeing geese in the area while being treated, bequeathed 12 more large geese of his own, adding to the flock. With the added birds, the semi-wild Silver Lake flock began to attract migrant geese as they passed through the area. Then, in 1948, a coal-fired power plant began to siphon water from the lake for cooling purposes, returning it five degrees warmer. The lake stopped freezing in the winter. Five hundred geese decided to make it their winter home, aided by food found in neighboring farm fields. For over a decade, their numbers increased.

Eight men showed up at Silver Lake on a blustery January day in 1962, to examine this unique flock that spent its winters so far north. Represented in that group were scientists from the Minnesota Department of Conservation (Forrest Lee, Bob Jessen, Tom Hanson, George Meyers); the Illinois Natural History Survey (Dr. Harold C. Hanson); and the U.S. Bureau of Sport Fisheries and Wildlife (Harvey Nelson, Art Hawkins, Bill Ellerbrock). After trapping a group of geese, the scientists set about examining and weighing members of the flock. Something soon seemed amiss.

When they weighed the geese, the men were dismayed. The weights were heavier than they should have been. Figuring that the scales were defective or affected by the frigid January air, Art Hawkins trudged off to a grocery store to make a purchase. He returned with a ten-pound sack of flour and a five-pound bag of sugar, first certifying their weights on the grocer's scales. With these sacks they tested their scales. The scales weren't defective. These were just darn big geese!

Dr. Hanson collected the skins of nine of the geese to take back to his laboratory as specimens. When Hanson compared the skins and measurements, along with the weight records that the men had gathered, to early records and skins of the thought-to-be-extinct, maybe-even-mythical giant Canada goose, he reached a stunning conclusion. The giant Canada goose had never been mythical, and it had somehow escaped extinction.

How did the geese escape their demise? In a fateful twist, the giant Canada goose survived primarily because of hunting. Across the midwest, hunters had captured some of the remaining wild local geese to breed, and to use as live decoys for attracting other geese as they passed south during the autumn. This practice saved the giant among Canadas from extinction. The geese adapted to domestication rather well, and the captive flocks prospered.

However, because live decoys were so devastatingly effective, the federal government soon banned their use for all types of waterfowl hunting. Some hunters kept their flocks because they were attached to them. Undoubtedly some geese were released or eaten. Others became the property of people interested in raising geese for a hobby, for sale to others, or as a cash crop. In any case, the giant Canada goose had survived, and by the time it was officially rediscovered, it was prospering in a few locations across its probable former range, from Tennessee north to southern Alberta. Though the bison were gone, changes in land use made it possible for geese again to find food, and those that had kept the geese as decoys had unknowingly perpetuated the race.

Because these geese were so easy to raise, and because surplus stocks were relatively easy to come by, Fish and Game departments, numerous sportsman's clubs,

and even towns and cities began in the 1950s to reintroduce the giant Canada goose broadly across the Midwest.

People were excited about the opportunity to restore this grand bird, and thrilled to see a symbol of wildness prosper in its former range. No longer would geese simply be a joy that passed quickly in the autumn or spring sky. Now they would be seen daily, and would live near us. Little did they know that, although a few big geese are a great thing, a lot of big geese can be a real problem.

Geese Too Many

Since its "discovery," the giant Canada goose has been stocked widely across the continent, from the Rockies to the eastern seaboard and south to Georgia. Many of these flocks are free-flying groups that migrate only short distances, and some don't migrate at all. There are flocks that abide in rural settings, and groups that have become urban dwellers. They're a mixed blessing. They bring the sight and sound of wildness to millions of people, enhancing our lives. But as their populations have grown in recent years, crop depredation problems in rural areas and nuisance complaints in the cities have grown as well. Dealing with these problems differs from location to location, from city to city, and from countryside to countryside.

The giants in the country are somewhat more easily managed, because the option of hunting remains open to wildlife managers. Though the solution sounds simple—reduce populations to an acceptable level through increased mortality—as we've seen, managing geese is never that straightforward.

In just about every instance where the giant occurs, it mixes with migrating flocks during the traditional hunting season. Encouraging hunting of resident birds while controlling the harvest of migrants is seldom

RIGHT: Ironically, the race of giant Canada geese was perpetuated when hunters saved a few of the remaining birds to breed for use as live decoys.

easy. A wide variety of plans have been tried. In some cases, a special season on the resident geese opens before the arrival of the migrants. These split seasons have generally been successful. The history of one flock of giants illustrates the technique.

Giant Canada geese were introduced into suitable habitat in west-central Minnesota in 1963 and 1964, near the towns of Fergus Falls and Alexandria. The Ottertail County and Douglas County goose refuges were established to protect the transplanted birds. A combination of excellent habitat and protection allowed the geese to prosper until, by the early 1980s, they had increased to such an extent that they were inflicting crop losses on area farms.

A two-year study indicated that the Fergus Falls flock should be reduced, then maintained at about 5,000 geese, and that the best way to increase mortality was to allow hunting. In 1982 a special five-day season was tried, but it failed to keep the population from expanding. At the same time, the Eastern Prairie Population of interior Canada geese (B.c. interior) was in decline because of poor weather in the nesting grounds. The daily bag limit of geese was reduced to protect these migrants from northern Canada. While effective in reducing the mortality of the migrant geese, the lowered bag limit also reduced the harvest of local giants, and the big geese continued to multiply.

In 1989, with the flock at an unacceptably high level, farmer complaints rose. Biologists feared an outbreak of disease in the overpopulated resident birds, which would then undoubtedly spread to migrants as they mingled. The U.S. Fish and Wildlife Service authorized the Minnesota Department of Natural Resources to experiment with a special season that would be held in early September, before most of the migrant geese appeared.

So far, after two experimental seasons combined with additional harvest during the regular goose season, the growth rate of this flock of giant Canadas seems to be slowing. The early season has also been successful in controlling mortality of the migrants—indications are that no more than six percent of the geese killed during the experimental seasons were found to be migrants.

Similar hunts have been tried elsewhere. Those yielding the best results in controlling resident goose populations are hunts that start before migrants arrive. In places where special late seasons were tried, or where the season was extended (after the migrants moved farther south), the harvest has not been so successfully increased. Most geese are killed during the first few days of the season, and hunter success diminishes rapidly as the season progresses. A little hunting pressure quickly educates these local flocks. Additionally, as autumn stretches into winter, fewer hunters venture afield in the increasingly inclement weather, and the geese make fewer feeding forays during cold periods. Under such conditions, hunters simply can't harvest enough of the crafty geese to lower productivity rates.

Undoubtedly, managers will further refine hunting seasons to better control local flocks while protecting other races of Canada geese. But large numbers of giant Canadas in need of population control remain in areas where hunting simply isn't feasible.

Wetside Story

Like an antagonistic street gang, they roam the cities, staking claim to what they consider "their turf." They're ready, willing, and able to drive out interlopers. They have no respect for private property, and they may physically threaten home owners. Gangs of them invade public parks and beaches, strut on corporate lawns, intimidate golfers.

Snow Flurries

Have snow geese responded too well to changes in winter habitat? Many biologists fear that there are now too many snow geese for their own good.

 The evidence is interesting. In recent decades, more and more snow geese have used migration corridors farther west during both their spring and fall journeys. The shift is apparently a response to abundant foods found in this corridor of intense agriculture, and these westerly concentrations continue to increase.

Historically, the majority of the mid-continent population wintered in the coastal marshes of Texas and Louisiana, and migration south was generally done in a nearly non-stop fashion. But infringement on the coastal marshes due to oil and gas development and levee construction left America's largest coastal marshes brackish or drained, seriously diminishing their value to geese.

The snow geese looked elsewhere, and found in the rice fields to the north an alternate place to winter. After a few years, they began to spend winters even farther north, wherever roosting water and agriculture coincided, much like Canada geese. During their migration, they also began appearing in large numbers in refuges that were formerly used only by Canada geese.

Apparently, the amount of quality wintering habitat has long been a limiting factor in snow goose populations. By utilizing a wider area in the winter, more snow geese can prosper, resulting in greater reproduction. The geese have also changed their migration patterns to take advantage of these new foods, migrating at a more leisurely pace and stopping much more frequently to feed and rest.

The resulting "snow blizzard" seems to have reached a near-crisis level. Ironically, the snow goose may have become too prosperous, and it now faces a dilemma. Evidence indicates that there are too many on the breeding grounds. Snow geese are returning to the arctic in poorer condition than ever before. Reproductive success rates are going down, and biologists fear that a crash is inevitable. The shorter migrations taken in short-distance hops may be out of necessity rather than preference. Because of overpopulation, the geese are leaving the northern nesting grounds in poor shape; they simply may not be capable of long-distance flights. The frequent stops along the migration route may be necessary breaks for rest and food.

Wherever they go they leave a mess behind, fouling areas to the point that the lands are unsuitable for public use.

Each year there are more of them—generations of youngsters recruited into the fold. They are big, boisterous, and practically fearless. Their "colors" are black, gray, brown, and white. They are urban Canada geese.

And yet these bullies are also a delight. Their feeding flights soothe the commuter stuck in traffic. Their song is a wild chorus that contrasts with the city's "civilized" cacophony. That they live with us is a blessing. That there are too many of them is not.

Urban geese are now a source of consternation for home owners, park and golf

OVERLEAF: Geese are now a common sight, even across an urban sky.

Adaptable and prolific, Canada geese have learned to live within a human-altered world.

course managers, airport commissions, and city councils from Denver to New Haven. First released into urban and suburban areas in the 1950s, Canada geese, primarily in the form of giants, now breed in Minneapolis-St. Paul, Detroit, Toronto, Wilmington, Boston, and several cities in Connecticut, New Jersey, and New York. In Minnesota's Twin Cities, there are now over 15,000 geese, up from only 448 in 1968. And because these geese are so remarkably adaptable, other communities will soon be faced with both the delight of year-round geese and the dilemma they pose.

Because geese are such highly social animals, the effect they have on an urban setting is not limited merely to a wayward goose dropping or two. Gathering in huge flocks and consuming large quantities of low-grade forage that quickly passes through their digestive system, geese foul beaches, lawns, docks, and golf courses to a degree that exceeds the tolerance of most urban people. Combine that problem with the threat to human safety when birds take up residence next to airports, interfering with air traffic, and it becomes clear that urban communities face a difficult wildlife management chore in a most unlikely setting.

Why do the geese do so well in the big city? University of Minnesota Professor James A. Cooper notes that these geese were

Urban landscaping provides geese with abundant forage in the form of grass.

actually predisposed to living in an urban environment. An urban setting with well-manicured lawns, ponds, and parks provides ample food, roosting sites, and nesting areas for geese. Since most other wildlife has been eliminated in the city, few if any natural predators threaten the urban geese.

Geese also seem able to ignore the hustle and bustle of the city, because of the way they evolved. Geese are group feeders, using the flock's many eyes and ears to warn them of trouble. But if geese erupted into flight every time one individual got prematurely nervous, they would not be able to feed effectively. Geese have therefore developed the ability to quickly determine what constitutes a threat and what does not. Golfers and picnickers are considered non-threatening, so the geese merely go about their business. When harassed by an angry home owner, geese learn to ignore the ranting person, seeing the commotion simply as an inconvenience because the harassment does not result in any adverse consequences.

What can be done? Should anything be done? Cooper explains that there are three options. We can decide to do nothing until the geese reach some type of natural limit. We can try through harassment to force them to move on. Or we can decrease the population through reduced productivity or increased mortality.

The first option seems impractical. Like all creatures, geese would eventually reach a population level that would stress their environment, resulting in disease or reduced reproductive success. However that level, estimated to be ten to twenty times more geese than are common now, would be far above the tolerance of most people. Many are already complaining about fouling or damage to landscape.

And as we've seen, harassment is seldom successful. Though it sometimes works in the short run, each time the threat is not backed up by repercussions, the wise geese simply learn to tolerate the inconvenience.

Sometimes mute swans are employed on ponds to drive geese away, since the swans too are territorial and become very aggressive toward the smaller geese. But a pair of swans can only expend so much energy in chasing geese. If there are many geese, the swans become ineffective. And swans can be a problem, too. They are much more prone than geese to attack people. There is one credible incident in which these big, aggressive birds assaulted a man alone in a small boat, pursuing him until he drowned. And mute swans, the only type readily available for "goose busting" duties, are not native to the North American continent. Further introduction of such exotics is not a thing that most wildlife managers believe should be encouraged. We're left, then, with the last option, that of reducing the population size.

Geese in urban settings enjoy a remarkably high survival rate of about 85 percent. A rate of only 50 percent is needed to maintain a population. Ultimately, lowering productivity is the only way to control urban geese. To lower productivity, though, you have to increase mortality or reduce breeding success rates.

The most traditional method of increasing goose mortality is through hunting.

But a hunt within a city is neither socially acceptable nor safe. An experimental hunt in the Minneapolis-St.Paul area, where the two big cities are ringed by rural farmlands, showed that of all the geese bagged, few were true urban and suburban geese—perhaps as few as one percent. Most urban geese simply never stray to outlying areas where hunting is allowed. They have far too much habitat readily available to them within the city.

Efforts have turned to either egg removal or destruction, techniques that mimic natural predation. If the eggs are removed, though, there's always a chance that the geese may initiate a second clutch. A more effective technique employs vigorous shaking of the eggs, killing the embryo. When the eggs are replaced in the nest, the goose will continue to incubate them until it's too late in the summer to lay a second clutch. But this is an expensive and intensive procedure, because thousands of nests must be located across a broad front.

One final option remains—the removal of birds during their flightless stage. After the goslings are large enough, and while the parents are still undergoing the molt, urban geese congregate. During this time it's possible to round up the flocks and remove them to another, more remote location. The technique is both successful and self-limiting.

First, because of the Canada goose's strong homing tendency, it's essential to transport the adult birds to a very distant location—preferably several states distant. Second, locations for release of both the young and old must be carefully selected, to avoid repeat performances of the same nuisance scenario. Few places are truly remote these days, and geese transferred to a rural lake may soon pose problems there for human residents, resorts, or public beaches. Translocation is ultimately self-limiting. All available habitat will someday be filled.

LEFT: Many Canada geese now winter in urban settings where food and water are available year-round.

However, at least when the geese are taken to remote sites, hunting can be applied as an additional controlling factor.

What will happen when translocation is no longer possible because the available habitat is filled? We will probably double our efforts to destroy eggs, and at least one biologist has suggested that surpluses from the ever-renewing resource of urban geese can be periodically captured and used to feed the urban poor.

From extinction to too many, from none to more than enough, from then to now, the story of the giant Canada goose is a fascinating one, full of conflict with humans from beginning to end. People caused their demise by disrupting the balance of nature; people kept the race from extinction by happenstance; and now people seek to control this adaptable bird that thrives in cities.

One can only admire the persistence and adaptability of the beautiful giant Canada goose. And it seems that they are having the last laugh. After all, if they make life difficult at times for humans, they're only repaying an old debt.

The Unending Story

Written by their marvelous migration, sung in honking chorus, the goose's story can help define for us a living history of our continent, and of life itself. From them we can learn of adaptation, of extinction, of recklessness and respect. Their prose is graceful, inspiring, emotional—and for that we love geese. When we listen to them, we hear a more primitive and natural rhythm— a composition wrought from sunrises and sunsets, seasonal migrations, and eternal faithfulness. Geese do what geese do: They eat, fly, reproduce, and die. They want only what they need, desire only to fulfill their destiny, and seek only habitats that nurture them.

Goose Busters

As the problem with the burgeoning urban goose population intensifies, a group of goose busters have emerged: Geese International.

Formed in Squaw Lake, Minnesota, in 1984, Geese International has as its mission the translocation of urban giant Canada geese to more pristine habitats in rural areas. Working with small translocations of four birds at a time, watched over by a human foster parent who is a Geese International member, their relocation strategy has been a success. Many of the geese released to date have been taken to the vast conifer and lakeland belt of northern Minnesota, a region many believed was unsuitable for Canada geese. But the geese have been prospering, reproducing and returning each year to their new home, raised from the status of urban nuisance to that of an admired symbol of wildness.

Through 1991, Geese International had transplanted over 5,000 Twin Cities-based problem geese to new sites in Minnesota and North Dakota. North Dakota is striving to establish a wild, breeding flock of giant Canadas in every county. Geese International works closely with the U.S. Fish and Wildlife Service and state wildlife agencies to ensure that releases are made in areas where the geese will not again become a nuisance.

The non-profit organization is seeking to grow into more states, to aid in the control of urban geese. Geese International can be reached at P.O. Box 225, Duluth, MN 55801.

RIGHT: Though an overabundance of urban geese can become a nuisance, geese also add to the quality of city life.

OVERLEAF: Geese possess a serene dignity.

For humans, prisoners of the plains who watch their winged passage, there is wonder at their grace, beauty, and hardiness. Nothing we know about geese—not all the science, not all the problems—can keep us from pausing in awe as great, powerful wings sweep gracefully through the sky. None of us but the most jaded can fail to appreciate the absolute majesty of geese. They possess a serene dignity. They do not ask questions or ponder the complexities of life. Since they know all that they need to know, they strive only to live life. They fly. They find food. They defend their territory and their young. To them death is no mystery, but an inevitability—temporarily avoided and ultimately accepted. In contrast to the manner in which we face our own lives, geese seem to be remarkably well-balanced.

Perhaps it's their fullness, their fitness for life, that we envy and that we hear in goose music as it passes on a starry night. In an accounting between our species and theirs, we are certainly the debtor. They have given us food, beauty, and music. We have dealt them mostly woe, our gift of grain merely a happenstance.

But we're learning. Geese now have many friends among bird watchers, hunters, scientists, organizations, and the general public. We realize our debt and seek to pay the geese their due. In the future, this will consist primarily of ensuring that they have access to the wetlands, tundra, and myriad other bits of habitat they need to survive. Through accident and ever-improving wildlife management, we have recently helped geese prosper. The accident of new habitat in which geese can winter speaks to the adaptable, indomitable spirit of the creature. The effort to learn more about geese and to help them prosper speaks to the generosity of our spirit.

If the goose continues to be lucky, and if we continue to get smarter, then ours is a relationship that will endure.

RIGHT: For these goslings, the future looks bright.

If you enjoyed **Wild Goose Country**,
be sure to ask for the other titles in our
"Wildlife Country" series:

Elk Country
by Dr. Valerius Geist,
photography by Michael H. Francis

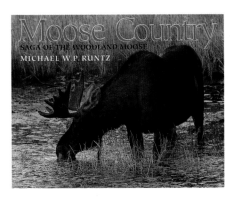

Moose Country
by Michael W. P. Runtz

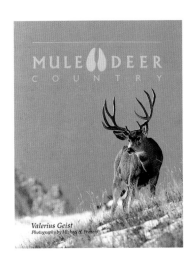

Mule Deer Country
by Dr. Valerius Geist,
photography by Michael H. Francis

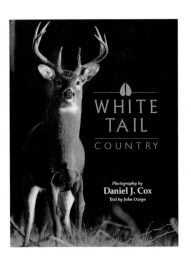

Whitetail Country
by John Ozoga,
photography by Daniel J. Cox

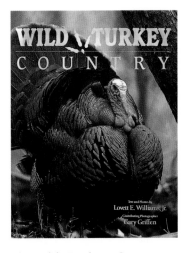

Wild Turkey Country
by Lovett E. Williams,
contributing photographer Gary Griffen

Published by NorthWord Press, Inc.
P.O. Box 1360 / Minocqua, WI 54548

For a free catalog of NorthWord products, call 1-800-336-5666